Exit Right

Achieving a golden goodbye by realising the maximum value for your business

Barrie Pearson

Published by Thorogood
10-12 Rivington Street
London EC2A 3DU
Telephone: 020 7749 4748
Fax: 020 7729 6110
Email: info@thorogood.ws
Web: www.thorogood.ws

A CIP catalogue record for this book is
available from the British Library.

HB: ISBN 1 85418 239 0
PB: ISBN 1 85418 244 7

Cover and book designed
by Driftdesign

Printed in India by Replika Press

To the memory of my late parents, Albert and Mary Pearson

Preface

The other alternatives available should be considered before deciding to sell a company. Grooming work needs to be done to ensure that the company is ready to be sold and to make it as attractive as possible to prospective purchasers. Timing the sale is important to get the best price.

Once a decision has been made to proceed with a sale, prospective purchasers at home and overseas must be identified. The aim is to identify those companies which will gain the greatest benefit, and so are likely to pay the highest price.

Competition is important to obtain the best deal. For the sale of subsidiary companies and divisions, formal auctions are being used more frequently. For a private company, an auction is much less appropriate, but competitive bidding must be achieved.

Valuation is a matter for truly expert judgement. Scarcity and rarity value, or strategic significance for a particular purchaser, must be recognised because these can enhance the price obtained substantially. None the less, realism is essential. Vendors often have inflated ideas of the worth of their company.

Negotiation is an art not a science. Acquisition negotiation is deceptively complex as well because of the legal and taxation implications. Earn-out deals are a potential minefield to negotiate. There are strong reasons for leaving the lead in the negotiations to be taken by advisers, not least because of the emotional involvement of the vendors. Once oral agreement has been reached, the sale must be carefully nursed through to legal completion.

Expert advice is essential. The choice is confusing. Investment and merchant banks, corporate finance boutiques, business brokers, chartered account- ants, management consultants and specialist advisers are possible sources of help and advice.

Loss making companies should be turned round into profit before sale. The effort and delay involved will be handsomely rewarded in terms of the price obtained for the company.

This book has been written to be of benefit to those business owners, group executives, accountants and lawyers who are likely to find themselves involved in selling a company. Equally, anyone involved in buying a private company will obtain a unique and invaluable insight into the way vendors and their advisers approach a sale.

A special thank you is appropriate to Claire Sargent, who made time to word-process the manuscript whilst doing a demanding job.

Barrie Pearson
Realization
Campbell House
Weston Turville
Aylesbury, Buckinghamshire HP22 5RQ

Contents

ONE
How to consider the options

Many owners of businesses think that the only options to consider are 'to sell, or not to sell'.

There are several other options which should be considered by prospective vendors, even if only briefly. These include:

- An earn-out deal

- A management buy-out or buy-in

- The sale of a minority stake

- A merger or acquisition, as a preliminary step

- A stock market flotation

- A transfer to the next family generation

Each of these options will be explained and assessed.

An earn-out deal

In a perfect world, a business would always be sold with payment in full at legal completion. More than half of all private company sales involve an earn-out deal, however, with some of the purchase consideration not only deferred but contingent on future profit performance. The reason is inescapable; purchasers want to protect themselves against poor performance if the business appears vulnerable. Some vendors are adamant that an earn-out deal is unacceptable, but many purchasers will simply not agree and withdraw.

An earn-out deal consists of the sale of a business for an initial sum and the opportunity to earn one or more subsequent payments based on the future performance of the company. Earn-out payments are usually based either on the annual pre-tax profit achieved in one or more financial years, or on the aggregate pre-tax profit achieved over two or three years.

Deals based on sales, gross margin or profit after tax are normally rejected by acquirers. The use of sales or gross margin would encourage the vendors to chase growth at the expense of profit. If profit after tax is used, there is the possibility that the amount of corporation tax could be reduced either by a change in the taxation rules or by the tax expertise of the purchaser, which means that the vendors would receive increased earn-out payments from circumstances outside of their influence.

An actual example of an earn-out deal is:

- an initial payment of £8.0 million

- plus £0.5 million provided that the profit before tax in the current financial year is not less than £1.25 million

- plus £0.5 million provided that the profit before tax in the following financial year reaches £1.5 million, and twice the amount of any additional profit up to a maximum of £2.0 million profit.

This means that the maximum purchase price to be earned is £10 million.

It must be realised, however, that there is no such thing as a typical earn-out deal. For example, in a case where the asset backing is particularly low and profit is expected to increase dramatically, the percentage of the total price to be earned by future profit performance may well exceed 50 percent, and in exceptional circumstances has exceeded 90 percent, of the total purchase consideration.

Expert tax advice is needed to ensure that an earn-out is structured tax effectively for the country in which the deal is to be done. Pitfalls to be avoided include the risk that the maximum capital gains tax will become payable on legal completion and the possibility that the deferred payments will be treated as earned income where this would increase the amount of tax to be paid.

Earn-out deals are commonplace, especially for service companies. The main reason is that private businesses are often heavily dependent on the personal contribution of the owners. In the case of a service company, because the net assets of the business may be only a small percentage of the purchase price, this becomes even more important to the purchasers.

Some acquirers underestimate the contribution of the owners, and do so at their peril. Key staff may have stayed with the business because of strong personal loyalty to the owners. Some important customers may continue to buy from the company because of a close acquaintance with the owners and the exceptional personal service provided by them. The goal to be achieved is a smooth transition from a privately owned business to part of a larger group without the unwanted loss of valued staff or customers.

In an earn-out deal, it is normal for the managing director to continue to manage the business throughout the period in which further payments can be earned. If for some reason the present managing director is unable to continue, perhaps because of ill health, then agreement should be reached with the purchasers that one of the other directors will manage the business. The owners will want to manage the business during the earn-out period in order to maximise the amount to be earned.

In most cases, earn-out deals should be arranged for only one or two financial years beyond the current year. This should provide adequate time to replace the owners. If an executive from the acquiring company is to understudy the present managing director for a period, the vendors should establish that the cost of the understudy will be borne by the acquirers to ensure that earn-out payments are not affected.

Sometimes earn-out deals are structured over five years. In the vast majority of cases, this is far too long. Acquirers must realise that the vendors will expect considerable freedom to manage the business throughout the earn-out period in a way which maximises the amount they will receive. This means that vendors are unlikely to pursue opportunities which will adversely affect their earn-out payment potential.

Some acquirers naively assume that because they do not envisage either diversification or the business making an acquisition itself, neither the need nor an opportunity will arise. Sometimes acquirers have become so dissatisfied with the former owners that they have chosen to attempt to negotiate their way out of an earn-out deal and found it an expensive way to gain management control of the business.

Vendors should realise that they are likely to find managing the business for new owners to be frustrating, and the thought of continuing for five years may seem like a life sentence.

The legal contract for the purchase of an unquoted company is likely to be at least thirty or forty pages of double spaced typing. With an earn-out deal the contract could reach one hundred pages or more, because there are numerous additional items which may need to be defined in the contract to protect both parties, such as:

- accounting policies and auditors
- management charges
- central services
- intra-group trading
- provision of finance
- dividend policy
- cost rationalisation

Each of these items will be explained, and illustrated where appropriate.

Accounting policies and auditors

On legal completion, it must be assumed that the company acquired will be required to change accounting policies to those of the group. This may reduce the pre-tax profits for the purpose of the earn-out deal. Also, the acquirer will wish the group auditors to replace the present ones on legal completion. So the profit figures set for earn-out payments must take into account the accounting policies to be adopted.

In a recent sale it was negotiated on behalf of the vendors that the accounts would be prepared by the present auditors using existing accounting policies during the earn-out period, and then converted into statutory accounts by the group auditors at the acquirer's expense. The reason for adopting this approach was because the advisers to the vendors felt that in this particular case, there would be too much scope for subjective differences in the application of group accounting policies, and the vendor's auditors were a major firm which provided some comfort for the acquirer.

Management charges

The policy of the acquiring company may be to handle centrally matters such as pension administration, payroll preparation and legal advice. Their procedure is likely to be to make a fixed management charge to each of their subsidiaries for the provision of these services, and the cost involved must be known and agreed, so that ideally there will be a cost saving which will increase the earn-out payment.

Central services

It may make sense for the acquired company to make use of central facilities such as the group delivery fleet for distributing goods; sharing the use of regional distribution depots; or using an in-house central media production department for website design and promotional literature. These services tend to be charged on a usage basis, and it is important to establish the basis and rate of charges which will apply during the earn-out period.

Intra-group trading

The acquired company may be an existing supplier to other subsidiaries within the group. Prior to the acquisition, goods and services will have been provided on an arms-length pricing basis. The acquiring company may have a group policy of 'artificial' transfer pricing between subsidiary companies, which could have a significant effect upon the profits of the acquired company. Equally, there may be a policy requiring subsidiaries to purchase from other companies within the group, even if a lower price could be obtained from another supplier outside of the group. Clearly, the vendor's advisers should negotiate to maintain the existing arrangements during the earn-out period.

Provision of finance

It is essential to establish that sufficient finance will be available to meet the expansion of the business required to produce sufficient profits for the vendors to benefit from the earn-out potential. If this finance is to be provided by the acquiring company, rather than by an overdraft from a bank, then the interest cost should be defined by reference to the bank base rate, and ideally should be at a lower cost than the existing borrowing facilities.

Dividend policy

It is unusual for an acquired company to be required to pay a dividend to the parent group during the earn-out period. None the less, this needs to be confirmed otherwise borrowings will need to be increased in order to meet dividend payments.

Cost rationalisation

Sometimes it will be agreed that some cost rationalisation will take place following the acquisition, for example the disposal of leasehold premises where two retail outlets would be located too near to each other as a result of the acquisition. It may be desirable to negotiate that all of the costs connected with the disposal will be borne by the acquiring company, so that if these are significantly greater than expected payments to be received under the earn-out deal are not adversely affected.

In the light of the above issues, it will be appreciated that an earn-out deal is much more complex to negotiate than an outright sale of the company.

Management buy-outs and buy-ins

A management buy-out involves members of the management team, backed by one or more institutional investors, buying the company which employs them. In the USA, management buy-outs are often described as leveraged buy-outs or LBOs, because the majority of the purchase price is provided by borrowed money rather than by share capital.

Management buy-outs are commonplace in the UK, continental Europe and the USA. In the UK, buy-out deals have ranged in size from several hundred thousand pounds to a billion plus, whilst in the USA, the size of the largest deals has increased to many billion dollars.

Management buy-ins usually involve a team of two or three executives, rather than one individual, buying a company in an industry sector in which they have experience, with the financial backing of institutional investors.

Suitable companies

Whether the acquisition is a buy-out or a buy-in, a large proportion of borrowed money will be used to finance the purchase. So there will be a heavy interest burden on the company at the outset. The ability to generate a positive cash flow is essential in order to reduce borrowings. This may involve the sale and leaseback of freehold properties; selling land for residential housing development; or disposing of part of the business as a going concern. Vendors need to identify and assess these opportunities before pursuing a buy-out or buy-in deal, and either set a purchase price accordingly or choose a different disposal route.

Companies with a high net asset backing as a proportion of the purchase price, even in a mature or unfashionable market segment, are often suitable because the assets are regarded as security for the borrowing required.

Some service companies are unsuitable for a buy-out or buy-in, because the low level of asset backing and uncertainty concerning future cash flow projections do not satisfy lenders. Businesses which are liable to require injections of cash are likely to be unsuitable, for example a high technology company which requires significant cash during the next two or three years to finance research and development.

Establish the price range

The first step should be to assess what price an acquirer may pay for the business and the likely market capitalisation if a stock market listing is a feasible alternative within the foreseeable future.

Even if a management buy-out or buy-in is an acceptable alternative, other prospective purchasers should be pursued first, or at least simultaneously, in order to ensure an attractive price is obtained.

Handling an approach

Sometimes a buy-in team will make an unsolicited approach to buy the company, 'backed' by a letter from a financial institution offering to support the purchase of a business up to a given value. It must be realised, however, that any institution invests strictly on the merits of a specific deal and any letter indicating support is far removed from a blank cheque.

A buy-out approach may be made without adequate thought or knowledge of what is involved.

Specific questions to be asked at the outset to those making a buy-out or buy-in approach should include:

- How much money are the team committed to invest themselves?
- How will they raise the cash?
- Has the MBI team had preliminary meetings with any financial institutions to discuss a possible deal?
- What purchase price range do they envisage?

Until satisfactory answers are given, the approach should not be allowed to progress further.

If the buy-out or buy-in is to proceed, the financial institutions will need to receive a detailed business plan. It needs to be established that:

- for a buy-out: if agreement to proceed is given, the team will write the business plan in their own time.

- for a buy-in: only limited time and access will be provided to obtain information needed to write a plan and a confidentiality agreement will be required.

When a financial institution has received the business plan and decides to proceed, the management team may be encouraged by them to seek a formal agreement to a period of exclusivity in which to pursue a deal. Further, the advisers to the management team may prompt them to seek a cost indemnity from the vendors to pay their professional costs up to a given limit if a deal is not completed.

Clearly, a period of exclusivity should not be agreed unless other alternative purchasers have been ruled out. Equally, any cost indemnity should be carefully defined and only entered into if it is appropriate.

Once a deal is underway, a timetable to legal completion should be agreed. It is unsatisfactory to allow undue delay because the distraction to the management team, together with the inevitable speculation and uncertainty within the business, is likely to impair performance.

The inevitable outcome

Financial institutions seek to realise their investment in a buy-out by a sale of the company or a stock market listing. The majority of institutions aim to achieve this within five years, sooner if possible.

Some vendors have felt cheated when the company has been sold or listed within only a year or two at a much increased valuation. This is another reason why the potential realisable value of the business must be assessed at the outset.

One other possibility which should be considered is for the vendors to retain an equity stake in the company after the buy-out or buy-in, in order to participate in any subsequent capital gain.

There is no room for sentiment regarding a buy-out. The management team should be regarded as merely another prospective purchaser. The potential value of the business should be assessed at the outset and any deal should be legally completed without undue delay.

The sale of a minority stake

Another option to consider is to sell a minority equity stake in the company to one or more financial institutions. This would raise some cash for the existing shareholders and they would retain management control of the business.

An institution is likely to wish to buy between 10 per cent and 40 per cent of the equity, and would want to avoid having more than 50 per cent of the equity.

Sometimes shareholders sell a minority equity stake or an option to purchase one without sufficient consideration, as part of an arrangement to obtain additional loan finance. Selling equity or granting an option in these circumstances should be regarded as a last resort. If the objective is to obtain loan finance, then every effort must be made to achieve it without disposing of equity on unfavourable terms.

A situation to be wary of is selling a minority equity stake to a competitor. Even before an equity investment is made, commercially sensitive information will have been provided. If the competitor is located overseas the information may be less valuable. Careful consideration must be given, however, before any options are granted to increase the investment to give majority control or outright ownership within a given period. Expert taxation advice is required to ensure that granting options will not crystallise any capital gains tax liabilities prematurely and that the risk of undervaluing the worth of the shares at some future date is minimised.

Valuation of a minority stake

It must be realised that the sale of a minority equity stake in an unquoted company of, say, 20 per cent is likely to be valued by a financial institution significantly lower than one-fifth of the price which may be realised by selling the whole company. Their reasoning is that a minority equity stake gives them little influence over the management of the company, even with the appointment of a non-executive director, and that the only opportunity to sell their minority stake may be to the other shareholders; unless the company is sold or obtains a stock exchange listing in due course. Consequently, it is important to approach three or four financial institutions at the outset to establish their interest and to obtain an indication of their valuation, before deciding to proceed in earnest with any one of them.

Appointment of a non-executive director

Institutions investing in the equity of an unquoted company will usually require the appointment of a non-executive chairperson or director nominated by them. The person nominated is likely to be someone from their 'pool' of non-executive directors or, possibly, an executive from the institution.

Unquoted companies tend to respond emotionally to the thought of having a non-executive director appointed by a financial institution on their board. It is not as bad as it may appear at first thought, and could prove helpful.

The institution should be asked to nominate someone who will add something to the skills of the board. For example, knowledge of the business gained from experience at either the supplier or customer end of the chain, or some relevant technical expertise, such as foreign currency management, if this is an important feature of the business. If the first person put forward does not appear to fit in acceptably, with board members, the institution should be asked to put forward an alternative candidate.

As well as carrying out a monitoring role on behalf of the financial institution, the non-executive director should be expected to bring a more structured approach to board meetings, offer a wider perspective on what is happening in the industry sector, and have some useful personal contracts amongst prospective customers and suppliers.

Eventual sale of the company

Many financial institutions will seek to realise their equity investment by a sale of the company or a stock market listing within about five years. If the wish is to obtain a long-term equity investment, then this should be discussed openly with prospective investors in the initial meetings.

One factor to be aware of is the possible problems created by having an outside investor when the time comes to sell the business. There have been cases where the financial institution has exerted considerable pressure to reject an offer which the remaining shareholders would have been quite happy to accept.

The sale of the minority equity stake may be an appropriate alternative if the objective is to release some cash for the shareholders whilst maintaining management control. It could be particularly appropriate if the goal is to achieve a stock market listing within the next five years, because the minority equity investment would accelerate the introduction of the disciplined approach required by a stock market listed company. The trap to avoid, however, is the sale of a minority equity stake or the granting of an option at a price which subsequent performance reveals was far too low.

Merger

There need to be strong reasons to justify two privately owned companies choosing to merge, which means that the two companies are joined into one without any exchange of cash.

Valid reasons

Some valid reasons to pursue such a merger could be to:

- accelerate a stock market listing by achieving the requisite level of profit more quickly;

- achieve the size of business required to support the minimum level of infrastructure needed to compete effectively, for example to afford the level of new product development required by a computer software company;

- reduce dependence on one product or service, or on only a few customers; or

- avoid the outright sale of a company on unfavourable terms arising from a death, serious ill health or enforced retirement.

Management

The future direction, priorities and aspirations of the merged business must be agreed at the outset, otherwise there is no point in pursuing a merger.

There is the strongest possible case for agreeing that there will be one managing director after the merger, and not joint ones, to avoid unnecessary disagreement. Both the principle and the choice of individual need to be agreed next.

The board members and their roles need to be agreed. Responsibility and accountability for particular functions such as marketing or sales cannot be shared effectively. One person must be given individual accountability.

Another issue which should not be underestimated is the problem of harmonising salary levels, fringe benefits and conditions of employment, without causing a significant increase in costs.

Also any relocation of offices or factory is likely to be time consuming and costly. Even the cost of a change of name should not be underestimated in terms of product literature, vehicle livery, stationery and so on.

Valuation

Failure to agree a valuation may well negate any real hope of achieving a merger.

The objective must be to agree the percentage of the merged company that each set of shareholders will own. This has to be achieved without the existence of a market price for the shares in either company to provide a benchmark.

Profit is almost certain to be the relevant basis, rather than net asset values shown on the balance sheets. The problem is likely to be, however, that the two companies will have different rates of profit growth, both to date and projected for the future. This means that disagreement is probable concerning the relative values of the two companies.

Overall, a merger of two privately owned companies should be avoided unless there are strong reasons for doing so. Even then, an acquisition of one company by the other, for shares or cash, may prove to be the only feasible alternative.

Stock market flotation

In the UK, there are two markets regulated by The Stock Exchange for companies seeking a quotation for their shares.

These are:

- The Official List

- AIM (Alternative Investment Market)

The main difference between the markets is the size of the companies whose shares are quoted upon them. So, the first requirement is to check that the profit of a company is suitable for a quotation.

The Official List

The Official List is the main market regulated by The Stock Exchange.

The value of the business on listing needs to be at least £100 million, and preferably more than £200 million.

AIM

AIM, the Alternative Investment Market, provides a listing for smaller companies.

In most cases, the value of the business on listing should be at least £50 million, in order to generate interest and an effective market in the shares, although smaller companies continue to join the market.

Suitable companies

It is not sufficient merely to have reported an acceptable level of profits to be a suitable company to obtain a share quotation. Suitable management and future profit growth must be demonstrated. There should be no serious question marks concerning the business or the directors.

The sponsors will have to be convinced that the company is suitable for a stock market quotation, because their reputation is at risk. They will want to be satisfied that:

- the company has a satisfactory record of profit growth during recent years; or a start-up business to be listed on AIM is sufficiently robust.

- adequate budgetary control, profit forecasting and cash management exist to ensure that current year forecasts are reliable.

- the profits will continue to grow at an acceptable rate during the next two or three years and the company has a long-term future.

- the company is not unduly dependent on one person, and there is demonstrable management competence.

- if the company has only one product or service, there is not undue vulnerability to changing demand or competition.

- the company is not unduly dependent on a mere handful of customers or clients.

- a suitably qualified accountant is employed as finance director.

- a medium-sized or large firm of chartered accountants are auditors to the company.

- the directors and major individual shareholders wish to continue their commitment to the company by retaining a substantial proportion of their shareholding.

- the corporation tax, PAYE and VAT affairs of the company are in order and up to date.

- adequate working capital is available for the growth and development of the business.

- there is no threat of major litigation hanging over the company.

Benefits of a share quotation

There are benefits to be gained by shareholders, directors and staff, including:

RETAINING MANAGEMENT CONTROL

The major shareholders will have the opportunity to sell up to about a quarter or more of their shares and still retain management control of the company.

ESTABLISHING A MARKET IN THE SHARES

A realistic market price will be created for the shares, which may be substantially higher than the prices at which occasional sales and purchases of shares have taken place previously. Also, small shareholders will be able to buy and sell shares more readily.

RAISING FINANCE

Additional avenues of raising finance become available. More shares can be sold in the future, probably by a rights issue to existing shareholders. As a quoted company, financial institutions will be prepared to underwrite a share issue so that there is no obligation upon existing shareholders to subscribe for additional shares.

As there is a market for the shares, the issue of more shares can be used to pay for acquisitions. Whilst it may be unacceptable for the vendors to receive the purchase consideration wholly or partly in shares, it should be possible to place blocks of shares with financial institutions to raise the cash required.

STATUS AND AWARENESS

Some private companies dealing with multinational customers and suppliers have a problem of financial credibility. There is evidence to show that a stock market quotation has been of significant help in creating an adequate financial status.

The press coverage leading up to a share quotation, and the continuing interest afterwards, is likely to increase awareness of the company significantly.

MANAGEMENT AND STAFF MOTIVATION

There is no doubt that the flotation of a company creates excitement amongst management and staff. There will be an opportunity for staff to buy shares at the time of flotation, or to sell a proportion of their existing holdings. A share option scheme should be introduced at the same time to create a wider involvement in the future success of the company.

Disadvantages of a share quotation

The amount of preparatory work involved and the continuing requirements for a quoted company should not be underestimated. The disadvantages of flotation include:

PREPARATORY WORK

The scrutiny of the company, and its future prospects, by the sponsors, or nominated adviser for an entrant on AIM, and the reporting account-ants is time consuming for the directors.

The reporting accountants will produce what is known as a long-form report examining:

- previous financial results for up to five years;
- the history, business, prospects, management and financial per-formance of the company and each subsidiary;
- management information and control systems, organisational structure and management succession;
- service contracts, pension schemes and benefits in kind;
- the forecast financial results for the current year; and
- the adequacy of working capital to meet the anticipated needs of the business.

The writing of the prospectus to accompany the share quotation must be the subject of meticulous attention to detail to ensure that the informa-tion is accurate.

It is desirable that only one or possibly two directors are closely involved with the provision of information for the long-form report and the prospectus. Otherwise, there is a real risk that the performance of the business will suffer during the vital period leading up to the flotation, which could undermine the achievement of the pre-tax profit forecast for the current year.

THE SIX-MONTHLY TREADMILL

In the UK, quoted companies are required to report their financial results for six-month periods. In the USA, quarterly reporting of results is commonplace.

Stock market analysts and financial journalists compare the results achieved for the first half of the financial year with the corresponding period in the previous year, as well as making a similar comparison for the full year performance. Without doubt, this does create additional pressure on the directors, management and staff of the business. Whilst capital expenditure and revenue expense need to be invested to ensure medium-term profit growth, there is still the requirement to produce an acceptable result every six months.

DIVIDEND PAYMENTS

As a private company there is no requirement to pay a dividend at all. For a quoted company, however, investors will have a definite level of expectation related to the size, type of business and future prospects of the company. It is quite typical for between one-third and one-half of profits after tax to be paid out as dividend to the shareholders in a quoted company. This is a significant drain on cash flow which cannot be ignored.

PUBLIC SCRUTINY

The directors of some private companies enjoy indulgences provided by the businesses which will be completely unacceptable to the sponsors. These may include a boat, an aeroplane or helicopter, an overseas villa, and racehorses. Some members of the families of directors may receive a salary and a company car, without having a commensurate job in the company. This sort of thing often amounts to using a company to finance an extravagant lifestyle, in a way which is totally unacceptable when outside shareholders are involved.

INFORMATION DISCLOSURE AND CONTINUING OBLIGATIONS

There must be timely disclosure of half-yearly and annual financial results to the Stock Exchange. Also, various other situations need to be notified.

Annual General Meetings have to become a formal and public occasion, requiring preparation to handle contentious issues which may be raised by those attending.

Directors are not allowed to buy or sell shares at various financially sensitive times during the financial year.

MEDIA ATTENTION

Journalists need stories, favourable and unfavourable. As a private company, it is probable that a story would not appear in the press at all, or only in local newspapers, and would not affect the share price.

For a publicly quoted company the situation is likely to be quite different. The sudden resignation of a founding director or the sale of a substantial part of a personal shareholding may not only be reported in the financial press but have a significantly adverse impact on the price of the shares as well.

DISSOLUTION WITH SMALLER COMPANIES

For several years now, there has been a growing and continuing trend for listed companies to be taken private. Market makers, the firms who trade the shares, and institutional investors have largely lost interest in investing in the shares of listed companies with a market valuation of less than £100 million. The rewards simply do not reflect the cost and effort involved compared with concentrating on larger companies.

As a result many listed companies below £100 million market valuation find that the share price undervalues them, and this applies to an increasing number of companies worth less than £500 million. Consequently, it is increasingly felt that the obligations and costs of maintaining a stock market listing are no longer justified.

A transfer to the next family generation

For some business owners, the thought of transferring ownership to the next family generation has a strong emotional appeal.

Some of the key issues to be addressed rigorously include:

- ability and aptitude;
- interest and commitment;
- other business opportunities;
- learning the business; and
- handing over the reins.

Each of these will be explained, and illustrated where appropriate.

Ability and aptitude

Emotional appeal is a nicety, financial reality is vital. Handing over the company to your children could reduce an asset worth millions drastically or even end up in receivership.

Relevant work experience can be acquired along the way, provided that the requisite ability and aptitude exist at the outset. A good test is to write down the educational standard and aptitudes required to be the managing director of your business, and then assess how well your children match up. Recognise that you may well have rose tinted spectacles, however, when assessing them.

A third generation business owner literally and deliberately brainwashed his two sons from being toddlers to join and eventually manage the family manufacturing firm; ability and aptitude were irrelevant. It had been a substantial and profitable business for decades, unfortunately it failed whilst the children were teenagers. The family lost their incomes and capital assets, so perhaps ability and aptitude were already lacking.

Interest and commitment

There is a huge variety of work opportunities for young people nowadays, so a key issue is whether or not your children are interested in business and, if so, have they shown a real interest in the company. They may be interested in business, but simply don't like your business sector. Real commitment, passion and hunger are crucial. If your children regard the business as a soft and lucrative option, the real danger is obvious. Equally, if they are lazy and quickly get fed up with things, these are tell-tale signs.

Other business opportunities

A mother had built up a successful executive recruitment business from scratch, but realised her son found the sector unattractive. He wanted to run his own business in the restaurant and hotel sector. She agreed to finance him, provided that he went to a top hotel school in Lausanne, Switzerland, and then learned his trade by working for a large group for a few years. Today, he owns a successful hotel in the south of France. This example makes the point perfectly, it may well be much better for everyone if you finance your children to start or to buy a business in a sector they really enjoy.

Learning the business

Assuming your children and you both agree it makes sense for them to join the family business, consider some of the recommended ground rules:

- Encourage them to get the best possible education, ideally including university.

- Don't rule out the possibility of your children qualifying as an accountant or a lawyer before joining the business.

- When they do join, make sure they learn the business at the nuts and bolts level, making sure they do not receive any favourable treatment.

- Consider encouraging them to join a major competitor, possibly working overseas, to gain a wider insight of the industry.

- Discuss the possibility of your children taking an MBA at a major European or USA business school.

Preparation for becoming the managing director needs careful planning over a five to ten year period.

Handing over the reins

Assuming the preparatory stages have been successful, probably the most difficult challenge remains, even if you truly believe your child is competent and ready to become managing director.

Your child should be either given a meaningful shareholding or helped to buy one, with the opportunity to become either a controlling shareholder or owner in due course. More important still, you need to really hand over the reins. There is a strong case for you to:

- give up your personal office;

- preferably leave the board immediately, and certainly within a defined handover period;

- resist any temptation to interfere; and

- offer to be available as a mentor, but only when requested.

To sum up, there are lots of success stories of handing over to the next generation but many more examples involving under performance and family bickering.

Executive summary

Consider alternative options to a sale:

- **Earn-out deals**:
    - require detailed negotiation and careful definition

- **Management buy-outs and buy-ins**:
    - regard the management team merely as another prospective purchaser
    - consider retaining an equity stake to share in future success

- **Sale of a minority equity stake**:
    - releases some cash and retains management control
    - realises less than pro rata price compared to outright sale

- **Merger**:
    - means no cash changes hands
    - needs strong reasons to justify it

- **Stock market flotation**:
    - requires a suitable business and management team
    - needs sufficient pre-tax profits to justify entry
    - shareholders must retain a substantial stake after flotation

- **Transfer to the next family generation**:
    - requires the requisite ability and aptitudes in your children, plus their real interest and commitment
    - needs careful planning over many years
    - most important of all, the parent must really step back completely

TWO
How to choose the time to sell

For private companies, the key issue is to decide when the owners wish to retire or exit from the business completely. Some people simply continue until they are ready to retire, wrongly imagining that once they have decided to sell a deal will not only have been completed within 12 months but they will have retired as well. This is certainly possible, but many people find the process takes much longer.

Owners of private companies need to look at least five years ahead of their planned retirement or exit date, because an earn-out deal may require five years from beginning to groom the company for sale, described in detail in Chapter 4, to being able to leave the business. Furthermore, this assumes that the climate to sell will be favourable when you want to sell.

The issues to be considered include:

- Timing risks
- Timing opportunities
- The overall time required

Timing risks

External factors such as the general economic climate, market sector prospects and acquisition activity will influence the saleability and realisable value of a company, and hence have a bearing on when to sell.

Although an acquisition should be a long-term and strategic decision, the current economic outlook influences buyer appetites. An economic downturn blunts the enthusiasm of corporate acquirers temporarily.

When a particular market sector is suffering a downturn, such as media services recently, despite a sound general economy, the likelihood is reduced acquisition activity and lower prices paid. Some private equity houses may be opportunistic buyers simply to make attractive investments.

Strong acquisition activity in a market sector may be followed by a lengthy lull because consolidation is nearly complete and companies concentrate on integrating their acquisitions. Any one of these external factors may mean that a sale should not be initiated until the climate becomes sufficiently favourable.

Companies which have been profitable for years, or even decades, may suddenly make a loss. The cause may be external, such as the loss of a major customer because it has been acquired and supplier rationalisation happened, but it will probably be necessary to delay a sale or make sense to do so. Many companies have a policy of never acquiring a loss-making business, unless it is to be integrated within an existing business and rationalised. Furthermore, the likelihood is that any purchase will be at a discount to tangible net asset value. If business failure is inevitable, however, urgent action must be taken to sell in order to salvage something.

A loss-making year is likely to delay a sale for up to two years. Buyers are likely to be cynical during the first profitable year fearing that the loss may have been overstated to create a more favourable return to profit. They are likely to want to see a profitable year completed, not merely forecast, and demonstrable, sustained profit growth in the subsequent year.

Another timing risk is the rapidly changing business climate which makes it difficult to foresee threats even three years ahead. Legislation, technological breakthrough, over-capacity in a sector, terrorist attack or a major public health problem may have severe impact on profitability. The threat of SARs, which had a major impact on airlines and hotels, temporarily appears to have subsided but a new and virulent flu virus is a real possibility. Frighteningly, too, tuberculosis appears to be spreading and some cases of bubonic plague have been officially reported, whilst the West Nile virus killed 277 people in the USA during 2002, and any of these has the potential to disrupt business drastically.

Serious illness is a real risk. People over 45, even those with a record of good health, face an increasing risk of an unexpected and sudden serious illness. If you are vital for the business, this could present a major problem to ensure management continuity, reduce the value of the business and even frustrate a sale.

Companies where sales have plateaued or profits are falling consistently may be unsaleable, because corporate acquirers are keen to buy businesses with the prospect of sustained sales and profit growth to enhance their earnings per share performance. If the future prospects for your business are declining and you do not have a deliverable strategy to revitalise performance, there is a strong case for selling sooner rather than later.

Timing opportunities

When a market sector is consolidating this is undoubtedly a timing opportunity, but you should recognise that a flurry of acquisition activity rarely lasts longer than two years, so do not miss the boat.

One sign of sector consolidation is when you suddenly become conscious of acquisitions being reported in the trade press. Another sign is if you receive two or three serious unsolicited approaches in quick succession, particularly if you have not received any during recent years. These signs merit talking to prospective corporate finance advisers to find out their assessment of acquisition activity in your sector.

Some owners believe that the best time to be negotiating a sale is when the audited accounts become available, typically three or four months after the year end. At this early point in the new financial year, prospective purchasers are likely to pay little heed to the full year forecast and base their valuation on the previous year's performance. Worse still, if the new year has started disappointingly they may be unsettled by the short-term prospects. A better time to negotiate a deal is as soon as the full year profit forecast is clearly achievable. This could well be three months before the year end and purchasers are likely to base their valuation on the forecast. It means that the same value may be obtained at least six months earlier because there is no need to wait for audited results.

The overall time required

The preparation time required to maximise shareholder value ranges from about three months to two years. A stock market listed company wishing to sell a subsidiary, should be able to complete the preparatory work within three months because adequate corporate disciplines and governance should be in place already.

For a private company however, there is a considerable amount of grooming work to be done in order to get the best possible deal. In many cases, grooming over a couple of years will deliver handsome rewards and most companies will require at least several months. The preparatory work is outlined in depth in *Chapter 5: How to Groom your Company for Sale*. So do remember to make adequate allowance in your overall exit timetable.

The transaction time, from initiating a sale to a legally completed deal and an exit for the owners varies according to the type of transaction.

Management buy-outs and buy-ins

Most management buy-outs and buy-ins require a transaction time of about six months, but some do drag on for about nine months because of setbacks during the deal.

Before giving permission for either an MBO or MBI to commence, however, a careful appraisal of trade buyers at home and overseas, and a realistic assessment of likely deal value and structure needs to be done. If appropriate, preliminary negotiations with selected prospective purchasers should take place before authorising an MBO or MBI. Alternatively, it may make sense for the management team to bid simultaneously with other purchasers in order to get the best deal possible. It does mean, however, an additional three months may be required for this appraisal before the transaction commences.

The good news for the vendors of a private company sold to a buy-out team, without any retention of an equity stake, is that usually they will be expected to leave immediately or after only a brief handover period. So it is entirely possible to achieve a complete exit within twelve months.

With an MBI, the new management team may need some part-time consultancy from the owners for a few months in order to achieve a smooth handover of customer contacts, technical expertise and any other invaluable local knowledge.

Outright sale to a trade buyer

An outright sale could offer the quickest possible personal exit for the vendors of a private company. The transaction time should be about six months, but could stretch to nine months if snags arise. If the business is to be integrated within a subsidiary of the acquiring group, the likelihood is that the vendors will be expected to leave on completion or after a brief handover period.

A typical transaction timetable for legally completing a sale to a trade buyer is:

Month	Action
1	• Write information memorandum • Research prospective purchasers at home and overseas
2	• Advisors approach prospective purchasers and obtain a signed confidentiality agreement before revealing the vendors' identity
3	• Meet prospective purchasers off-site • Arrange a visit to company premises for short-listed purchasers
4	• Receive written offers, clarify offers and negotiate improvements • Select preferred purchasers • Negotiate and sign heads of agreement
5	• Due diligence takes place • Legal contracts drafted and negotiated
6	• Legal completion takes place and consideration is paid on completion

Some vendors of private companies assume that a sale to a trade-buyer will enable them to be paid in full and exit the business within six to twelve months of initiating a sale. The reality is, however, that at least a half of private company sales to a trade buyer involve an earn-out deal, and it is naïve of vendors to imagine that a categoric refusal will achieve them an outright sale. Instead, it may rule out any chance of a sale.

Earn-out deal

The transaction time required for an earn-out deal should be similar to that for an outright sale.

The period of executive involvement by the vendors after legal completion will be significantly longer, however, than in an outright sale. This is particularly likely to be the case if:

- the asset backing is less than, say, about 25 percent of the aggregate purchase price; and/or

- the future success could be adversely affected by the loss of one or more major clients; and/or

- the business is significantly dependent upon the personal expertise or contribution of one or more of the vendors; and/or

- there is inherent uncertainty about the future profits because of outside influences such as possible legislation or major technological development affecting the industry sector.

Most earn-out deals extend for one or two years beyond the current financial year. In exceptional cases, however, the earn-out payments have extended over five years but vendors should reject this as too long, and not accept more than a three year earn-out period.

Executive summary

- Assess your planned retirement or exit date at least five years ahead.

- Identify and assess timing risks which could delay or undermine a sale.

- Spot timing opportunities and capitalise on them if appropriate for you.

- Recognise that grooming work to obtain the best possible deal will require from a few months up to a couple of years.

- The transaction time is likely to be about six to nine months.

- Realise that more than half of all companies sold to a trade buyer involve an earn-out period of usually one or two years, and occasionally three years.

THREE
How to choose and use professional advisers

Outside help is costly, and there can be no guarantee that a deal will result. Despite this, however, external advisers are commonly used by private companies and many listed groups, because they lack the technical knowledge, relevant experience and management time needed to ensure a successful deal. Private company owners will find that selling a business is a prolonged emotional roller coaster, with the added stress that the deal may collapse shortly before anticipated completion.

In order to decide what outside advice and help may be needed, or beneficial, it is necessary to identify the tasks to be done and the expertise required.

The tasks to be done include:

- identifying the options available, both now and in the foreseeable future;
- choosing the preferred option to pursue;
- grooming the company to obtain the best deal possible;
- carrying out tax planning;
- valuing the business;
- deciding the target price to seek and the minimum to accept;
- writing an information memorandum to sell the opportunity;
- identifying prospective purchasers or investors as appropriate;
- approaching them to establish a definite interest;

- negotiating the deal and ensuring maximum tax efficiency; and

- handling the legal work to complete the deal.

Relevant professional advisers are:

- a corporate finance adviser or business broker;

- solicitors; and

- tax advisors.

Existing advisers should be considered first because they should understand the company and hopefully some rapport and chemistry already exists. It cannot be taken for granted, however, that the auditors and present solicitors will have the requisite experience.

Each firm should be asked:

- Is there at least one partner who specialises in corporate finance or at least is involved regularly?

- What deals has the person completed during the past twelve months? How large and complex were these? Who were the advisers to the other side?

- Is it possible to meet the person concerned? (Unless he or she is already known.)

Each type of advice will be considered in turn.

Corporate finance advisers

It is not essential to use a corporate finance adviser, even though they are widely used by private companies and listed groups. The benefits should be weighed against the costs involved.

The role and benefits delivered should include:

- dispassionate advice on the saleability of the company, the timing of the sale and the likely range of realisable value;

- reviewing the activities of the company to identify any obstacles to a sale and to recommend the action required;

- identifying a shortlist of known serious buyers from around the world with most to gain from the acquisition opportunity;

- writing an information memorandum to sell the opportunity to the key decision-maker of each prospective purchaser;

- hosting and chairing the initial meetings with prospective purchasers to confirm their interest and to agree what further information will be provided in order for meaningful written offers to be submitted;

- receiving written offers, negotiating improvements and clarifying any ambiguous aspects or material items not included;

- negotiating any earn-out involved to maximise the proceeds for the vendors;

- negotiating Heads of Agreement for maximum tax effectiveness, writing the 'Heads' with the purchaser and agreeing a detailed timetable to legal completion;

- steering the deal safely to legal completion, which typically takes six to ten weeks from signing Heads of Agreement;

- enabling the vendors of a private company to concentrate on managing their business with minimum distraction to ensure that the current year profit forecast is achieved; and

- acting as a 'buffer' between the vendors and prospective purchasers to avoid or defuse heated situations, which may well happen in a management buy-out.

The real job of the corporate finance adviser, however, is to obtain the best possible deal for the vendors with an acceptable purchaser. In this way, their fee should be repaid several times over by the enhanced deal they achieve for the vendors.

Corporate finance advisers work on a shared risk fee basis. They charge a commitment fee, which is capped, for doing the work involved and out of pocket expenses. They receive a substantial success fee which should only be payable on legal completion. This means that a failure to achieve a sale will leave them poorly rewarded, but a legally completed deal will give them a handsome reward.

Some corporate finance advisers will ask that the commitment fee should be paid in full before they commence work, and this should be flatly rejected. Payment should only be made for measurable progress and ideally a fixed amount would be payable when:

- the information memorandum has been completed;

- the list of prospective purchasers to approach has been agreed; and

- the first written offer has been received, preferably in excess of an agreed figure.

If the project is aborted for any reason, or put on hold temporarily, there should be no obligation to pay the full commitment fee. The amount to be paid should reflect the progress made to date.

Typical success fees are:

Deal value (£ million)	Successful
4	3%
10	2%
25	1.5%
100	1%

A trap to avoid is that the success fee should be payable at legal completion based on the deal value including the maximum possible earn-out payments. This should be rejected, and fees should be payable only when the purchase consideration is paid or the maximum earn-out payment should be reduced to 50% for calculating the deal value if the whole fee is to be paid on legal completion.

Corporate finance advisers often propose an inverted success fee scale because vendors like to feel that there is a real incentive to get the best possible deal.

Case Study: Inverted fee scale

The vendors said that £7 million is the lowest acceptable deal value, and agreed with their corporate finance advisers that £9 million is a realistic goal and it may be possible to exceed £10 million. As an alternative to a success fee of $2\frac{1}{4}$% plus a commitment fee of £30,000, the advisers proposed an inverted success fee set out below:

Deal value (£ million)	Inverted fee
Up to 6, plus	$1\frac{3}{4}$%
Over 6 to 8, plus	4%
Over 8 to 10, plus	7%
Over 10	10%

Comparison of fee payable		
Deal value (£ million)	$2\frac{1}{4}$ scale fee (£'000)	Inverted fee (£'000)
7	157.5	145.0
8	180.0	185.0
9	202.5	255.0
10	225.0	325.0
12	270.0	525.0

This inverted fee scale is loaded in favour of the adviser because at the minimum acceptable deal value of £7 million the fee is only £12,500 lower but at the realistic figure of £9 million the fee is £52,500 higher. The highest fee level should be 7 1/2%, but some vendors have accepted a top level of 15%.

A more acceptable inverted fee in the above case would be:

Deal value (£ million)	Inverted fee
Up to 7, plus	2%
Over 7 to 9, plus	4%
Over 9 to 12, plus	5%
Over 12	7½%

Comparison of fee payable		
Deal value (£ million)	2¼ scale fee (£'000)	Amended inverted fee (£'000)
7	157.5	140
8	180.0	180
9	202.5	220
10	225.0	270
12	270.0	370

At the lowest acceptable deal value of £7 million, the vendors save £17,500 and at the realistic figure of £9 million the advisers earn an extra £17,500, which is equitable, and the prospect of a substantially greater reward far exceeding a realistic deal value.

Whilst the case study is an actual situation, it should be regarded as purely illustrative. The key message is that vendors should be ready to negotiate both the threshold levels and the percentage fees payable in each band.

Corporate finance advisers may be categorised as follows:

- corporate finance boutiques
- accountancy firms
- investment banks

Each will be considered in turn.

Corporate finance boutiques

Boutiques come in different shapes and sizes. Many countries have scores of them, but quality and experience differ widely. To be competitive on fees, most boutiques set a minimum success fee equivalent to a total deal value of from £3 million to £5 million. Some claim to handle deals up to £100 million, but this is often a dubious boast. It should be tested by asking:

- What is the largest deal you have completed in the last year?
- How many deals have you completed in the past twelve months and what is the average deal value?

It is unusual for a boutique to have an overseas office, so their track record of selling businesses to overseas purchasers must be tested. A few are members of worldwide networks, which should help them to find overseas buyers, but it is important to establish that network members work solely for the vendor and share the fee, rather than another member acting for a purchaser and collecting another fee which could present a conflict of interest.

Accountancy firms

Major firms have corporate finance departments in cities and large towns worldwide. Some offices only handle deals worth at least £10 million, and their regional offices may accept deals from £5 million upwards. So it is important to choose a firm who will view your deal as attractive for them to handle.

Although they have a worldwide network of offices, check that fee sharing happens when an overseas office finds the purchaser. Otherwise, there is no incentive for overseas offices to help.

Second tier accountancy firms typically have a specialist corporate finance department in capital cities and some limited presence elsewhere. They handle deals worth £5 million plus and are competitive with the boutiques on quality of service and fee levels.

Small accountancy firms welcome corporate finance work because of the prospect of lucrative fees. Unless they have at least one partner working full-time on acquisitions and disposals, however, it is unlikely that they have the requisite experience. Sickness and holiday cover may be inadequate, and the ability to research overseas buyers may be modest.

Investment banks

Many banks have minimum deal sizes ranging from £50 million to £250 million or more, so they are unsuitable for the vast majority for disposal of private companies.

Business brokers

Brokers generally handle deals up to about £3 million. In Europe, including the UK, business brokers tend to offer only an introduction service between buyers and sellers. In some ways, this may be compared with the services provided by the traditional estate agent.

It must be understood that the fee basis most business brokers adopt in the UK is 'no deal – no fee'. Even more significant, they usually expect to receive their fee from the purchaser, although they have been appointed by the vendors to sell their business.

This must motivate business brokers to:

- encourage people to sell their business rather than pursue other options; and

- accept an offer even though it may be possible to find a better one.

It should not be assumed that business brokers are experts in valuation, taxation or negotiation. Positive proof is required. It is uncommon for business brokers to be involved in the negotiation at all. Most business brokers assume the stance of the nice guy in the middle 'who does not take sides'. Furthermore, prospective purchasers have a marked tendency not to want business brokers present during negotiations. In one instance where the broker suggested negotiating on behalf of the vendors, the prospective purchaser said 'I am happy to pay your scale fee for a completed deal but I will not have you present to act against me'.

The 'no deal – no fee' approach may make brokers look attractive, but some of them gossip. They are keen to tell as many people as possible which businesses they are selling, not only to find purchasers for a particular company but to convince people that they have a large number of businesses for sale at any time. Gossip can damage a company which is for sale if the information travels back to either employees or customers. Strict confidentiality must be expected and demanded of any adviser connected with a disposal, and business brokers should be reminded of this.

Brokers typically send out literally hundreds of anonymous descriptions of a business for sale, usually one to four pages long. Prospective purchasers will be required to sign a fee agreement in order to learn the identity of the company, but many do this just to satisfy their curiosity, and typical fees are:

- 5% of the first £1 million, plus
- 4% of the next £1 million, plus
- 3% of the next £1 million plus
- 2% of the next £1 million, plus
- 1% of the balance

Some purchasers will negotiate a lower fee, which makes them a less attractive purchaser for the broker.

A few brokers charge a fee to both the buyer and the seller, which should be flatly rejected because it is double-charging.

Solicitors

Most private companies need to use a firm of solicitors occasionally and groups may have an internal legal department, but this does not mean that either is equipped to handle a disposal because it is markedly different work from property, litigation or general commercial matters.

The solicitor needs to work full-time on acquisitions and disposals to have sufficient experience. A partner in a medium-sized firm should be capable of handling deals up to £50 million, and will charge significantly less than a major international firm. Most cities and large towns have at least one suitable firm to use, and are likely to charge less than solicitors in a capital city.

Two situations involve additional demands. If the purchaser is likely to use a major international law firm it is important that your solicitor has successful experience of dealing with major firms. It is a fact that some solicitors are overawed by a major firm and will concede more than they should. If your business is to be sold to a management team, it is vital that your solicitor has ample previous experience of buy-outs and buy-ins. The transactions are more complex, involve additional issues, and there will be separate firms acting for the equity investor, the debt provider and the management team.

Some solicitors may offer to save you money by negotiating the deal so that corporate finance advisers are unnecessary. Generally, solicitors do not have relevant experience to negotiate a deal and are unlikely to be able to find buyers internationally.

Tax advisors

Many entrepreneurs have a personal tax adviser, which may not be part of the audit firm. If the personal tax adviser has adequate relevant experience to handle the tax issues arising from a disposal, it makes sense to use them because they know your entire tax history. A new adviser will have to charge you for learning your history because tax considerations must reflect your overall situation.

Capital gains tax rules on company disposals change almost annually, and often recent precedent cases have an important bearing on the application of the rules. So it is vital that your tax adviser has current full-time involvement with disposal work.

Some vendors naively think that their situation is straightforward and tax advice is an unnecessary expense. This is nonsense. A disposal is pregnant with tax issues to be addressed in order to minimise the capital gains tax payable and it is strongly recommended to obtain 'tax clearance' by the tax office prior to legal completion, to give the vendors comfort that the deal appears to be structured acceptably.

How to pick advisers

The first step is to identify, say, three prospective firms to meet. The tried and trusted method of asking business acquaintances for suggestions is an obvious starting point. Trade press magazines may contain articles or case studies written by advisers, and news of completed deals may name the advisers involved. Internet search and reading websites is another source.

If you are unsure which individual to contact, telephone the personal assistant to the senior partner and ask who is the relevant partner to handle the size, complexity and business sector of your deal. When you speak to the person, outline your needs and the agenda you wish to address when you meet. For a corporate finance adviser, the agenda should include:

- the recommended exit route and timing;
- the names of known or likely buyers;

- the probable deal value range; and

- the disposal process and fees involved.

At the meeting, questions to be asked of any professional adviser include:

- What transactions of similar size and complexity have you completed in this market sector or a similar one?

- May I have the name, job title and telephone number of three clients for whom you have completed deals, if I decide in principle to appoint you?

- Will you be present at every meeting I want you to be?

- What will happen if you are on holiday or ill?

- Who else will be in your team and what is their role?

- What is your fee proposal?

- May I have a copy of your standard letter of engagement as well as a written proposal?

Questions to be asked of previous clients include:

- Did the adviser personally lead the team for you and attend meetings when you felt it appropriate?

- Did you get an outstanding deal, first class service and value for money?

- What things annoyed or irritated you?

- Would you unhesitatingly appoint the adviser again?

- How should I get the best out of the adviser?

- How enjoyable was it to work with the adviser?

Chemistry and style are truly important, this will become apparent during long, tedious and contentious negotiation meetings.

Executive summary

- Use existing advisers, provided they have the relevant experience.

- Corporate finance advisers are not essential, but are widely used by private companies and listed groups.

- Beauty parade, say, three prospective advisers to appoint one.

- Ask searching questions of prospective advisers.

- Expert legal and tax advice are always essential, there is no such thing as a straightforward deal.

- Take up telephone references from previous clients of your lead adviser.

- Always have a written fee proposal and an acceptable letter of engagement before appointing an adviser.

- If either the fee or the terms of engagement are unattractive, negotiate changes.

FOUR
How to groom your company for sale

Houses need grooming for sale in order to obtain the best price, and so do companies.

When selling a home, a modest amount spent on redecoration and minor repairs makes it look more attractive and cared for. When selling a company, the grooming must be much more than a few superficial cosmetic improvements in order to get the best possible deal.

Whilst some vendors decide to exit and quickly achieve an outstanding deal, most companies can be made more saleable and achieve a substantially better price by careful grooming which may take from three months up to a couple of years, or even longer in exceptional circumstances.

The preparatory work involved in selling a company can be categorised as follows:

- Essential preliminaries
- Optional preliminaries
- Deciding what to sell
- Good housekeeping
- Separating out a subsidiary or division
- Enhancing value for the shareholders

Each of these categories will be described in detail.

Essential preliminaries

Circumstances which are likely to dissuade prospective purchasers from buying the company or will cause inevitable delay need to be resolved before it is offered for sale. It is naive to think that a purchaser will not discover them during the 'due diligence' investigation work prior to legal completion. Worse still, by then significant cost will have been incurred and the staff may be unsettled by rumours that the company is being sold.

Potential barriers to a sale include:

- litigation;
- warranty claims;
- problems with the tax authorities;
- planning uncertainties affecting land and property; and
- compliance requirements of regulatory bodies.

In general, the likelihood, threat or even possibility of one of these situations arising, and the consequent uncertainty, is more off-putting to a prospective purchaser than if the full extent of the problem is known.

Each of these potential barriers will be considered in turn.

Litigation

Probably the majority of companies are involved in or faced with the possibility of some kind of routine litigation at any time. Examples include the pursuit of monies owed to or by the company, and perhaps an unfair dismissal case. These are unlikely to prove to be a barrier to the sale of the business.

Litigation which could be commercially damaging or expensive to resolve may well prove a hazard. One actual case involved a building products company which had recently entered the US market. An American company claimed that the company's major product infringed their patents and that they would take vigorous action to stop further sales in the USA. A dispute of this kind may take years to resolve and may well render the company temporarily unsaleable.

Warranty claims

If a new product has been launched on a large scale and serious design or manufacturing faults have been discovered, then there could be substantial warranty claims to be faced in the months ahead. Fortunately, in such a case, it should be possible to estimate fairly accurately the anticipated warranty costs in excess of the standard provisions included in the accounts, and to demonstrate that the fault has already been eliminated in subsequent production.

Tax problems

An investigation in progress by the tax authorities, or the threat of one arising in the light of preliminary enquiries, understandably unsettles a prospective purchaser. It is far too glib to assume that because the vendors will be required to give comprehensive indemnities concerning taxation, the problem need not concern prospective acquirers. Purchasers are well aware of the professional cost and management time involved in handling a tax investigation, and are likely to be concerned that other problems may be raised.

Issues which may cause serious tax problems include such mundane matters as benefits in kind for directors and senior staff, and the payment of people on a self-employed basis when they should have been treated as employees.

The only possible advice to anyone envisaging selling a company at any time in the future is to handle all the tax affairs impeccably from the outset.

Planning uncertainties

Planning uncertainties affecting land and buildings can be either negative or positive, but both may affect the sale. A negative uncertainty concerned a freehold building on the outskirts of a major city which had a 'trade counter' and parking for customers along the front. As part of the 'due diligence' investigation work, it was discovered that the planning authorities had prepared a provisional scheme for a motorway spur road to be built which would lead to the loss of the 'trade counter' and parking facilities. Even though it was only a provisional scheme, and other alternatives were being considered by the authorities, the purchaser withdrew from the deal because of the uncertainty involved.

A positive uncertainty concerned the possible opportunity to redevelop a large site, and to relocate the business locally without the loss of key staff. The vendors offered written evidence that planning permission would eventually be obtainable and gave examples of the prices obtained for similar residential development sites in the city. Not surprisingly, prospective purchasers were not prepared to pay a price for the business which reflected the redevelopment potential value. The vendors were faced with relocating the business first, in order to eliminate the uncertainty to a prospective purchaser, extracting the original site from the company and selling it for redevelopment at a later date.

Compliance requirements

European Union legislation has affected many companies. For example, some food production companies have needed to invest substantial capital expenditure to upgrade their manufacturing premises and equipment or to change their product specification. Prospective purchasers will want to be satisfied that forthcoming or anticipated legislation requirements are being addressed, and that the requisite capital expenditure and impact on production costs has been included in budgets and medium-term forecasts.

Recent major financial scandals have lead to a tougher and more costly regulatory framework, and some pensions and investment providers face the threat of claims for miss-selling which may take years to resolve and are difficult to quantify in the meantime.

Optional preliminaries

There are two main option preliminaries, namely:

- vendor due diligence; and

- public relations (PR).

In many cases, the pros are far outweighed by the cons and so each will be considered in turn.

Vendor due diligence

For most disposal deals worth less than £50 million, vendor due diligence is a waste of money, consumes the vendors' precious management time and delays the sale process. Despite this, the corporate finance departments of major accountancy firms sometimes push this service as a means of maximising their fees.

A vendor due diligence report is usually carried out by a specialist team of a major accountancy firm. The aim is to give prospective purchasers a comprehensive picture of the business. If material issues of a legal, environmental or pensions nature are involved, other experts may need to be involved.

Vendor due diligence is carried out before marketing the company to prospective purchasers and it is likely to be at least three months before a purchaser signs Heads of Agreement, and wishes to carry out their own due diligence. Purchasers tend to be sceptical about vendor due diligence, and profit forecasts will be somewhat dated, and so it will not speed up legal completion.

When a company is to be sold by a publicly announced control auction, vendor due diligence is often appropriate. Quite rightly, private companies reject announcing a sale and are keen to maintain confidentiality as long as possible. Controlled auctions are appropriate for corporate subsidiary disposals, however, usually valued in excess of £50 million where the group is confident of achieving a sale at an acceptable price.

Public Relations (PR)

Many private companies make no effort to gain media coverage in either the trade or national press, on the grounds that it costs advisory fees and management time for little benefit. Some private companies use PR advisers, however, to generate additional profit and regard media coverage as a profitable investment.

Sometimes, an adviser will recommend seeking relevant press exposure 12 months before initiating a sale in order to raise the company profile. New product or service launches, major contracts won, successful customer project completions, awards won and senior executive appointments are likely to gain coverage. It is not a clear cut decision, however, and the cost and management time involved needs to be weighed against the expected benefits.

What to sell

Matters which need to be considered, and resolved where appropriate, include:

- Directors' other interests
- The ownership of property used by the business
- Overseas companies, including dormant ones

Each of these will be considered in turn.

Directors' other interests

A purchaser will need to be satisfied that there will be no conflict of interest after the sale. For example, the directors may be shareholders in a related business, which could compete to some extent with the business to be sold or create confusion amongst customers if a similar trading name is involved. Alternatively, a director may own and have a part-time role in a quite different business. If the purchaser requires the full-time executive involvement of the director in the business to be sold, then this potential conflict will have to be resolved.

In deciding what to include in the sale, the rule must be to avoid any possible conflict of interest after the disposal.

Ownership of property

In private companies, it is not unusual for properties used by the business to be owned by the shareholders as individuals, as part of their tax planning. As the company and the property are owned by the same individuals, it is quite normal that neither formal lease nor rental agreement exists for the use of the property by the business. An open mind should be kept whether or not to include the sale of the property with the business.

For example, if the value of the property is likely to increase substantially because planning permission may become possible for housing or retail development, then it may make sense to offer only a medium-term lease to the purchaser of the business.

Purchasers tend to become nervous when overseas property is involved. They will want satisfactory evidence that the title is owned by the company. If this cannot be established, then it could affect the sale of the business. It must make sense whenever buying property overseas to ensure that the legal work is handled professionally and that adequate evidence of title is available.

Overseas companies

Some companies register overseas subsidiaries in order to protect the use of the company name. Perhaps some of the subsidiaries do not actually trade. It may seem attractive to a vendor not to sell one of these because it may provide an opportunity to establish overseas residency for tax purposes and to have a continuing business interest as well. It must be recognised, however, that a prospective purchaser will wish to avoid any conflict or the inability to use a valuable trading name in another country.

Good housekeeping

The lack of good housekeeping is unlikely to present a barrier to the sale of a company, but it may cause some delay. The existence of it, however, is an indication of professional management and is likely to be reassuring to a purchaser.

The elements of good housekeeping include:

- Shareholder agreement to sell
- Share structure
- Taxation affairs
- Accounting policies
- Employment contracts
- Incentive schemes
- Intellectual property

Each of these will be considered in turn.

Shareholder agreement to sell

A purchaser will usually wish to be satisfied that 100 per cent of the equity is available to purchase. Alternatively, if only a tranche of the equity is to be purchased initially, the purchaser may insist on an option to purchase the remainder. So it is essential to obtain the agreement of all the shareholders to sell their shares. If some of the shares are owned by a financial institution they may only agree provided that a given price is obtained, and one which may not be at all easy to achieve. If some of the equity is held in a trust, then extra time may be needed to obtain the requisite agreement to sell, especially if it is based in an offshore tax haven. If one of the shareholders has died without leaving a will, or probate of a will has not been granted, this may cause delay.

It is a necessary preliminary step to obtain the agreement of all the shareholders to the sale of the company.

Share structure

The best share structure to have for the sale of a company is simply one class of ordinary shares. Whenever there are different classes of ordinary shares, with different rights attached, there is a risk of disagreement. The different classes of shareholders are likely to have conflicting views concerning the relative values of each class.

So it is desirable to reach agreement about relative values before the company is offered for sale, and anything which is done to simplify the share structure helps to avoid disagreements at the negotiation stage.

Taxation affairs

Purchasers are reassured when all the taxation affairs of the company are up-to-date, in correct order, and the approval of the tax authorities has been obtained for computations submitted.

This applies to all tax affairs including:

- Corporation tax
- Capital gains tax
- Employee income tax
- Overseas profits and income
- Dividends received and paid
- Benefits in kind for directors and senior staff

There is merit in always ensuring that all tax affairs are kept up-to-date continuously, but perhaps this is a counsel of perfection. One thing is certain, however, as soon as a decision to sell the business has been taken then strenuous efforts should be made to bring the tax affairs up-to-date.

Accounting policies

It must be realised that as soon as the sale of a company is legally completed, a purchaser will install common accounting policies. Furthermore, it is completely naive to assume that a purchaser will be fooled by accounting policies which artificially inflate profits, for example the use of extended periods for the depreciation of fixed assets. Purchasers usually restate the profits of the target company using their own accounting policies as part of their valuation calculations. So there is no benefit to be gained by choosing accounting policies to artificially inflate profits.

Employment contracts

In many countries, legislation requires that each employee has a written contract of employment. Some private owned companies ignore this requirement but it should be complied with as part of their preparation for a sale of the company.

Incentive schemes

Some private companies have individual incentive schemes for directors and senior staff which may be totally unacceptable to a large purchaser. In an electronics company employing about one thousand people, the twelve most senior people had personal incentive schemes which they had negotiated individually with the principal shareholder and chairperson. Furthermore, the schemes were open-ended and ill thought-out. For example, the group marketing director received a bonus calculated as a fraction of one per cent of total sales, payable even if the company made a loss. Also, no provision had been made to exclude sales resulting from the acquisition of another company. The purchaser insisted that these incentive schemes were 'bought out' prior to legal completion.

Intellectual property

The administration of intellectual property such as patents should be in order and up to date. Patent renewal deadlines should have been met so that adequate patent protection exists. Wherever appropriate, patents should have been applied for in the overseas countries where trading takes place.

Separating out a subsidiary or division

Several months may be needed to arrange the affairs of a subsidiary or division so that it can be separated out easily and cleanly.

The issues which need to be addressed include:

- Premises
- Use of central services
- Pension entitlement
- Use of intellectual property

Each of these will be described in turn.

Premises

There may be various situations which need action. The premises may be owned by a property subsidiary of the group and leased to the business to be sold. A decision must be made whether or not to sell the premises, taking into account the potential increase in value in the foreseeable future and the crystallisation of any capital gains tax liabilities by selling now. Another possibility is that the business to be sold shares the premises with another subsidiary which is to be retained. The use of the space may make it extremely difficult to separate the two businesses effectively. It may be preferable to offer the business for sale on condition that it is relocated within, say, twelve months, but some purchasers could find this unattractive or even unacceptable.

Use of central services

Some central services can be transferred more quickly and easily than others when a subsidiary or division is sold. Routine matters such as payroll preparation and pension administration fall into the 'easy' category. A dependence on an integrated information systems technology capacity may well be difficult to transfer quickly, especially if the software used by the purchaser proves to be incompatible.

It is unrealistic to think that the information technology issues can be resulted until a particular purchaser is in sight. The preparation which should be done before then, however, is consideration of a reasonable handover period and a basis of charges for services provided in the meantime.

Pension entitlement

The pension fund assets and liabilities relating to those staff who are to be transferred on the sale of the business need to be calculated by a firm of actuaries, or by an insurance company if they manage the group scheme. This is likely to take quite a while and instructions should be given sufficiently early to ensure that legal completion is not delayed.

Use of intellectual property

There may be certain patents, brand names, copyright and other intellectual property owned by the group, which will need to be transferred. This should be relatively routine but a complication may arise if the intellectual property is also used for the benefit of other subsidiaries which are to be retained by the group. Some form of licence will need to be drawn up.

Enhancing shareholder value

The most important preparation work to be done is that designed to increase the financial benefit to the shareholders.

Amongst the aspects of the business requiring adequate preparation prior to disposal are:

- Full asset valuation
- Full profit declaration
- Evidence of rising sales and profits
- A business plan
- Cost reduction and deferral

- Undue customer dependence

- Management continuity and key staff retention

- Surplus or unwanted assets

- Surplus cash

- Overseas expansion and diversification

- Acquisitions

- Effective management information

- Directors' pensions

- Future salaries for directors

Full asset valuation

Properties may not have been valued for several years and be undervalued on the balance sheet. Whilst purchasers will usually base their valuation of the business on profits and cash flows, you should point out the current market value of any property because this effectively reduces the goodwill or premium over the net asset value for the purchaser.

Formal property valuations are expensive and not necessary for this purpose. You should simply seek to get a current value by researching local commercial property valuations or obtain an informal opinion from a friendly property surveyor.

Full profit declaration

Stock and work-in progress may be valued conservatively by private companies in order to minimise the corporation tax payable. One method is to provide generous stock provisions in the accounts. This has particular significance for the value to be obtained by shareholders, because an important determinant of the price to be paid for a business is the profit after tax of the business.

A simplified example will illustrate the significance. Assume that the stock and work-in progress are undervalued on the balance sheet at the time of sale by, say, £300,000. If this is merely pointed out to the purchaser it will have little or no impact on the price offered. The benefit is likely to be treated merely as increasing the net asset backing as a percentage of the purchase price.

Now consider if the £300,000 were to be released into the profit and loss account during the previous financial year, the current year and the next one. This would increase the annual pre-tax profit by £100,000. If the corporation tax rate is 30 percent, the increase in profit after tax will be £70,000. If the purchase price were calculated on, say, ten times post-tax profit, this would increase the value of the business by £700,000.

The message is clear. Do not understate profits in the lead-up to a sale of a business.

Evidence of rising sales and profits

The natural concern of any purchaser is the risk of buying a business which has reached a plateau, or worse still, is about to decline.

The desirable pattern to demonstrate is:

- Sustained sales and profit growth during the previous three years.

- A further improvement for the current financial year.

- Evidence of another increase during the following year as a result of business development already in the pipeline, such as new products, branch openings or overseas expansion.

- Profit margins being maintained or improved.

So it is important to demonstrate rising sales and profitability of the business in the two or three years prior to the sale.

Business plan

When a group is disposing of a business, prospective purchasers will be keen to read the current business plan. Whilst projected sales and profit forecasts may be viewed with considerable scepticism, the narrative describing opportunities and business development projects to be pursued will be read with considerable interest.

Relatively few privately owned companies take the trouble to produce a written business plan for the next three years. If one exists, however, it will be looked on favourably by prospective purchasers. If not, the vendors and their professional advisers must adequately describe and sell the business development opportunities to prospective purchasers.

Cost reduction and deferral

Many purchasers value a business as a multiple of annual profits, so the profit for the previous and current financial years are vitally important. In the case of an earn-out, the forecast profits for the two following years will materially affect the structure and amount of deferred purchase consideration payments.

Wherever possible, indulgent expenses should be deferred such as:

- redecorating premises;
- re-carpeting offices; and
- refurbishing the car park and such like.

Equally, discretionary expense should be reviewed and reduced wherever possible, without damaging the performance of the business such as:

- advertising;
- corporate hospitality; and
- medium or long term research and development projects which will only benefit the new owners.

Surplus or under-performing staff should be removed humanely and generously, otherwise the purchaser is likely to do so and may treat people less generously.

Undue customer dependence

One customer or client may account for more than 50% of the total gross profit of a successful company. The loss of the customer, or even dual sourcing with another supplier, would plunge the business into losses. Some purchasers would find the degree of vulnerability too great, and others would insist on an earn-out linked to key customer retention. If the customer is acquired by another company, supplier rationalisation often happens and the account could be lost even though service performance has been satisfactory.

At least two years before initiating a sale, every effort must be made to reduce the dependence by winning other major accounts or diversifying into an adjacent market segment.

Management continuity and key staff reduction

Unless the business is loss-making or is to be absorbed into another subsidiary of the acquiring group, the purchaser will want an established managing director to continue. Appointing yourself as chair person and promoting someone to general manager or managing director shortly before sale will fool no one. You need to demonstrate that you have stepped back for at least a year and handed over key roles, such as business winning, successfully. Better still, you may have already reduced your involvement to part-time.

The loss of your managing director or a key team of software designers shortly before initiating a sale may cause you to delay a sale or will reduce the realisable value. Even if your key people are well paid, there is always the risk that someone will offer more. Share options may persuade people not to be tempted, but it is important that people cannot cash in their options on leaving because this could incentivise them to go rather than to stay.

Surplus or unwanted assets

Surplus assets, such as equipment and surplus or redundant stock should be sold, or scrapped if necessary. Cash flow is improved, more space for expansion by the new owners is created, and a better visual impression of good housekeeping is created as well.

Surplus cash

A cash generative business is attractive to purchasers, but it is not necessary to leave surplus cash on the balance sheet. At the outset, tell prospective purchasers that either the business will be sold on a cash and debt free basis or only with sufficient cash for current year working capital needs. If you only mention this later, the purchaser is likely to say that their valuation assumed the cash would be left in the business and so they need to reduce their offer by the amount of cash to be taken out.

Overseas expansion and diversification

Diversification or overseas expansion are likely to incur losses for at least a year and provide a management distraction as well, which will reduce the value of the business to a purchaser. Some vendors naively believe that the future prospects will encourage a purchaser to pay handsomely for them, but until profitability has been demonstrated this is improbable.

Acquisitions

Shrewd acquisitions can enhance realisable value but timing is important. Purchasers are acutely aware acquisitions often perform less well than expected and this may not become apparent during the first twelve months. If an acquisition is material, then ideally the performance should have been proved during a complete financial year before initiating a sale of the enlarged business.

Future salaries for directors

If an earn-out deal is involved, the directors will be keen to keep their salaries low where there is a benefit to be gained under the agreed formula. For example, if the earn-out payments are to be five times the profit before tax over a target figure in the current and following finance year, the lower the directors salaries are set the more they stand to gain from the earn-out payment.

If an outright sale takes place, however, then it is in the directors interests to negotiate the best possible reward package if they are required to enter into a service contract to manage the business for a period for the new owners. It may be possible to negotiate a profit-related bonus in addition to the basic salary to be paid.

Effective management information

A well-managed business, either privately owned or part of a listed group, should have annual budgets, reliable monthly management accounts produced promptly, and current financial year forecasts of sales and profits updated regularly. Mere opinion of the likely sales and profits for the current financial year is likely to be viewed with scepticism.

The production of budgets, prompt monthly accounts and updated year-end forecasts is sound business. So it makes sense to introduce these well before a sale is intended.

Directors' pensions

In the two or three years prior to a sale, or at least during the year of sale, consideration should be given to the benefit for directors of the company making substantial lump-sum payments to a personal pension scheme, especially if the directors have not made adequate pension arrangements for themselves. From a purchase price standpoint, there should be no adverse impact because a purchaser should 'add back' the pension payments as these will not be a continuing cost.

Executive summary

Preparatory work falls into several categories:

- Some problems, or even potential problems, need to be resolved prior to sale. They include:
    - litigation
    - warranty claims
    - investigation by the tax authorities
    - compliance requirements of regulatory bodies
    - planning uncertainties affecting land and property
    - legislation affecting produce specification or production facilities

- What is to be sold needs to be decided, including:
    - directors' other interests
    - ownership of property used by the business
    - overseas subsidiaries

- Good housekeeping which needs to be done before selling includes:
    - all the shareholders agree to the sale
    - relative values of different classes of shares agreed
    - taxation affairs and computations agreed and up-to-date

- Separating out a subsidiary or division requires:
    - sale or lease of property to be decided
    - transfer of central services to be considered, especially information technology
    - calculation of pension fund assets and liabilities for staff to be transferred
    - transfer or use of intellectual property to be arranged

- Enhancing shareholder values should involve:
    - full asset valuation
    - full profit declaration
    - evidence of rising sales and profits
    - a concerted drive to maximise profits

FIVE
How to handle unsolicited approaches

Prospective vendors have a marked tendency to act first and think later when receiving an unsolicited approach; or making one to a prospective purchaser themselves. In both cases, careful thought is essential.

Unsolicited approaches fall into two categories:

- approach by an intermediary; and
- direct approach by a prospective purchaser.

Each of these situations will be considered separately.

Approach by an intermediary

An approach may be received from:

- an investment or merchant bank;
- a firm of chartered accountants;
- a corporate finance boutique; or
- a business broker.

A bank will almost certainly be acting on behalf of a specific client. Chartered accountants and corporate finance boutiques are likely to be acting for a specific client, but this should be confirmed at the outset. It is always possible, however, that the client is your own management team finding out if you are prepared to consider a sale. Some business brokers may give the impression they are acting for a specific purchaser, but they are working entirely on a contingent fee basis and the acquirer is unaware of the companies being approached. Alternatively, the broker may simply be seeking prospective vendors. In every case, caution is essential.

An approach by letter

If there is a definite intention not to sell the business in the foreseeable future, a sensible course of action is simply to throw the letter in the waste-paper bin. Another would be to file it in a deep drawer.

None the less, curiosity may come into play. There may be a desire to find out who wishes to buy the company or what the business might be worth.

If so, the response should depend on whether or not the approach was made by a well-known firm of advisers. If not, the first thing to ask for is a written list of the deals they have completed in the previous twelve months, naming buyers, sellers and deal values.

Their business address may give some indication about them. An address which is a street in a small town suggests an individual operating from home. An unlimited company in the UK suggests a small business. Cowboys do exist. It is essential to be satisfied that the intermediary is a reputable company.

The next step should be to establish by a telephone call:

- the name of their client company;

- the name and job title of the individual in the company they are working for, and a telephone number to verify the approach is legitimate;

- if the client asked them to make specific approaches;

- if not, why the particular company was selected for an approach and how much knowledge of your business they can demonstrate; and

- what basis of reward the intermediary is working on, which could be purely speculative on a no deal – no fee agreement or a specific fee for making a systematic search plus a success fee on legal completion.

The answers to the above questions, or lack of them, will give a clear indication of whether it is a carefully targeted approach on behalf of a specific client or merely a general approach within the business sector to find companies to sell. At this stage, it should be made clear that the business is definitely not for sale.

It is quite possible, and reasonable too, that the intermediary is only prepared to name the client at a meeting. This could well be at the request of the client to avoid disclosing their acquisition intentions unless some degree of interest, rather than curiosity, is shown. If a meeting is to take place, then a visit to the intermediary is recommended because the offices are likely to reflect their substance.

An approach by telephone

Telephone approaches have become more commonplace. If the name of the intermediary company is not a familiar one, it may be appropriate to ask for the approach to be made in writing, together with a list of deals completed during the previous twelve months. Then pursue it as described already for dealing with a written approach.

If there is a definite intention not to sell, however, then it is best to end the telephone conversation as soon as possible, making it quite clear that the company is not for sale.

Meeting an intermediary

A meeting with an intermediary, as a result of an unsolicited approach enquiring if the company is available to purchase, should only take place provided that:

- full details of the prospective purchaser has been given; or
- will be given at the beginning of the meeting.

The approach during the meeting should be to disclose the minimum of information about the company, and to find out as much as possible about the prospective purchaser and the intermediary. At the end of the meeting, it should be made clear that the company is not for sale or that further thought may be given to the approach, whichever is appropriate.

If there is any wish to pursue a sale, then the next step should be to appoint advisers to provide expert guidance and to identify other known serious buyers at home and overseas.

Direct approach by a prospective purchaser

The approach may be made by a person already known to the directors. Alternatively, it could be by telephone or letter from an unfamiliar company.

Even if the approach is from someone already known, the response should be either a reluctance to sell or a statement that the company is definitely not for sale in the foreseeable future. Information about the business should be given sparingly.

If the approach is from an unfamiliar company, the first step should be to check that it is a company listed on a stock market or a company which has a private equity shareholder keen to provide the funding to make acquisitions. If not, a credit status check will establish, at the cost of a few pounds, the size and purchasing power of the company.

Another type of approach, but a less frequent one, is from individuals wishing to pursue a management buy-in. This requires a cautious approach. It is reasonable to ask for written details of:

- their career to date;
- the amount of their own money available; and
- evidence of the willingness of a financial institution to back them.

Unless this information is really convincing, then a meeting should definitely not take place.

Your own management team may request the opportunity to carry out a management buy-out. Even if you are sympathetic to the idea or would like to pursue it, great caution and immediate professional advice is required.

Meeting a prospective purchaser

Resist any suggestion that the prospective purchaser should visit the company for an initial meeting. One of your own staff may have worked for the prospective purchaser or recognise them from photographs in the trade press. The possibility may be remote, but the danger is that it would trigger gossip and speculation.

The meeting should take place either at the offices of the prospective purchaser or on neutral ground, such as a restaurant, provided that confidentiality is assured.

Once again, the posture should be one of reluctance or curiosity. Little information should be provided. The aim should be to find out the intentions of the prospective purchaser. The information to be obtained includes:

- The authority of the individual making the approach.

- What higher level of approval is needed before a written offer can be made.

- The commercial rationale underlying the approach.

- Which other companies are being approached.

- How much they know about your company.

- How they intend to expand or rationalise a company acquired.

- Whether an outright purchase or earn-out deal is envisaged.

- What management continuity they want.

- The criteria used to decide how much to pay for a company.

- What timescale to complete a deal is envisaged.

This information will give a valuable insight into the importance and urgency of their acquisition plans. The questions need to be asked in a low-key way, however, in order to avoid giving the impression of a willingness to sell.

It may well be suggested that the next step is to visit your company. This should be politely and firmly resisted.

If the approach has triggered a desire to explore a sale, the next steps should be to:

- decide a sale is the preferred option;

- consider if it makes sense to sell now; and

- meet prospective corporate finance advisers and appoint a suitable firm to act for you.

Some vendors wait until they are ready to have final negotiations with the company which approached them before appointing advisers. This cannot make sense.

Several weeks will be required to approach other prospective purchasers and progress to the stage where other companies are ready to negotiate. In the meantime, there may be considerable pressure from the company which made the approach either to negotiate a deal and give them exclusivity, precluding your talking to other prospective purchasers, or to terminate the discussion.

Before making an approach to prospective purchasers

Recognise the risk you are taking. You may be convinced that your business would be the ideal acquisition for a particular company, or the chief executive may have mentioned in the past that they would be keen to do a deal whenever you decide to sell. It does not mean, however, that the company wishes to acquire your business today. If you mention a possible exit, even indirectly, there is nothing to prevent the company from telling other people. Worse still, if the company is a competitor they have an incentive to leak the information to your customers, even if this does seem improper.

Unsolicited approaches to prospective purchasers should always be made by corporate finance advisers, without revealing your identify until they have been confirmed as serious buyers.

Executive summary

Remember a sensible approach is simply to say the company is not for sale.

Unsolicited approaches include:

- A letter from an intermediary:
    - if no intention to sell, simply ignore it
    - be satisfied it is a reputable company
    - confirm it is acting for a specific client
    - arrange any meeting on their premises
- A telephone call from an intermediary:
    - ask for written confirmation before considering it, unless you know the intermediary is a reputable firm
- A prospective purchaser making direct contact:
    - from a known person – be guarded
    - from an unfamiliar company – check their financial status
    - a buy-in team – check their credentials and financial backing
    - a buy-out team – request time to consider it and take expert corporate finance advice before responding

Meet a prospective purchaser on neutral ground and ask penetrating questions.

Before making an approach to a prospective purchaser:

- recognise the risk you are taking; and
- use a corporate finance adviser to avoid disclosing your identity until they are established to be a known serious buyer.

SIX
How to value a business for sale

There is no right answer for the value of an unquoted company, whether it is privately owned or a subsidiary of a group, and it can even be argued that the only meaningful valuation is the highest amount which one of several known serious buyers is willing to pay.

None the less, it is possible in most cases to calculate the likely price range which can be achieved with an acceptable degree of accuracy.

For owners of private companies, it is not enough simply to assess the likely purchase price of the business. The amount to be obtained by an executive director, after paying capital gains tax, may not be sufficient to finance early retirement. Yet for a person of, say, forty-five, it may be difficult or simply unattractive to make a new career or to start another business permitted under the restrictive covenants imposed by the purchaser. So the loss of annual income needs to be weighed carefully against the capital sum to be obtained.

Executive directors of private companies are not in the habit of calculating the annual cost of sustaining their present life-style out of capital. Yet the calculation must be made.

Consider someone aged forty-five who enjoys a lifestyle which costs about £125,000 a year net of income taxes as an executive director. Assume the sale of the company would require retirement from the business after one year. If the amount to be received for the individual shareholding was only £1.5 million net of capital gains tax, this would not necessarily sustain the existing lifestyle to normal retirement age, even ignoring the impact of inflation. Also, the pension to follow would be reduced substantially because of the premature termination of pension contributions.

People tend to underestimate the cost of maintaining a lifestyle enjoyed by the executive directors of a private company. In addition to salary, other benefits to take into account include:

- The purchase of a car and all motoring expenses

- Another car which may be provided for a spouse

- Any dividends received

- Opportunities for combining business with pleasure, such as foreign travel and eating out

- Pension contributions paid by the company

- Any other fringe benefits

It is not unusual for the total cost of these items to exceed the net of tax salary received.

The fundamentals of valuing a business

The price any purchaser is prepared to pay is likely to be determined by the profit and cash flow produced from owning the business, and to a lesser degree by the balance sheet worth of the assets.

The importance of adjusted profits

Purchasers of a business usually produce adjusted profit figures for at least the previous financial year, the current one, and two future years.

To value a business on behalf of vendors requires a similar approach, and the professional advisers should present adjusted profit figures to prospective purchasers at the outset.

From the vendor's standpoint it is worth adjusting profits for the previous three years if this will help to establish a record of rising profits. One-off events which may have significantly reduced profits in a year include:

- A large bad debt as a result of a major customer going into liquidation
- The costs of relocating a factory, warehouse or office
- A strike affecting deliveries from a key supplier
- The costs arising from major litigation
- The closure of premises or the termination of a product
- The start-up costs associated with entering an overseas market
- Significant redundancy costs
- Lump-sum pension contributions for directors

Additionally there may be other factors which will enhance profits for the new owners, such as:

- the directors being required to accept a reasonable executive salary after the sale, compared with the substantial rewards enjoyed as owners and directors;
- the intention that a director will retire upon the sale of the business and will not need to be replaced;
- the savings arising from the termination of relatives working for the business at inflated salaries;
- the benefits to be gained from recently taken action such as a price increase, the elimination of a loss making activity; and so on.

It is particularly important that the profits for the previous financial year and the current one are adjusted to show the most favourable picture which can be portrayed accurately.

In the case of the disposal of a division or subsidiary, it is important to adjust the profits by 'adding back' charges allocated by the present group which will cease following a disposal. These include a wide range of possible allocated costs such as:

- a group management charge based on a proportion of central staff costs;

- a percentage levy based on sales value for group expenditure, such as research and development or public relations;

- service charges for the use of central departments such as informational technology, payroll and pension administration; and so on.

The reality is that the acquiring company should be able to provide the resources required at a much lower incremental cost than is presently allocated by the existing group. Equally, it must be realised that the overall impact on the profits of the existing group will be significantly larger than the profits reported by the subsidiary. The reason is that in practice it will not be possible to reduce group costs by the amount allocated to the subsidiary. For example, the sale of a subsidiary is unlikely to reduce commensurately the amount which needs to be spent centrally on research and development or public relations.

Equally, if the aim is to make a realistic assessment of the worth of a business to a purchaser, it would be naive for the acquirer to ignore the extra costs which will be incurred.

Examples of the extra costs which will be taken into account by a prospective purchaser are:

- the appointment of a qualified financial controller to replace an unqualified bookkeeper;

- the need for increased insurance cover;

- increasing some salaries to avoid unacceptable differentials compared with similar staff already employed within the group; and

- additional pension contributions arising from employees joining the group pension scheme.

The acquiring company will take into account opportunities for increased profits as a result of acquiring the business. It is equally important that these are quantified by the vendor as well. Typical opportunities to increase profits are:

- Purchase cost savings as a result of increased purchasing power

- Cross selling the products and services of the acquired company to existing group customers, and vice versa, both at home and overseas

- The rationalisation of premises and overhead costs

The aim must be to negotiate a purchase price which reflects a share of the additional value created by the profit opportunities arising from the acquisition to be enjoyed by the vendors.

Cash flow projections

Purchasers will be concerned to make detailed cash flow projections, probably for at least two years forward, as part of the valuation exercise. Vendors should prepare at least outline cash flow projections as an important part of their own valuation.

Factors which need to be taken into account include:

- the amount of cash to be generated, or injection needed, based on the expected business growth;

- the need for capital expenditure to replace existing assets or to refurbish premises;

- capital expenditure to meet the planned expansion;

- the cash proceeds arising from the sale or redevelopment of surplus assets; and

- cash balances in the balance sheet at present.

When acquiring a service company, on an earn-out deal spread over several years, the cost of deferred payments may be generated out of cash retained by the acquired company. If this type of situation is not quantified, the company may be sold at too low a price.

If there is surplus cash in the company, consideration should be given to the possibility of using it for the tax-effective benefit of the owners, by making lump-sum pension payments or paying a pre-completion dividend.

In a similar way, cash to be generated by the disposal of surplus assets after the sale must be reflected to some degree in the purchase price. One example is the opportunity to dispose of an office because the acquirer has vacant space nearby.

Adjusted balance sheet worth

The most recent and audited balance sheet should be adjusted to reflect the current net asset worth by taking into account:

- the market value of freehold premises; and

- retained profits since the balance sheet date.

It has been explained in Chapter 4, that understated current assets such as stock work-in progress and debtors should be adjusted through the profit and loss account, and in the balance sheet as well.

Valuation criteria and factors

Adjusted profits, cash flow forecasts and present balance sheet net asset worth need to be calculated rigorously.

The recent financial performance, current and future year forecasts will be carefully scrutinised by the acquirer as part of the due diligence. Although a deal will have been agreed and reflected in the signed Heads of Agreement by this stage, vendors must be aware that if a shortfall in current year forecast performance looks likely then a lower price will be negotiated. On the other hand, it is important not to understate the current year profit forecast or this will reduce the original offer, so a careful balancing act is required.

It would be wrong to assume, however, that an accurate valuation can be made simply by arithmetic application of financial criteria or formulae. Less quantifiable factors must be taken into account as well.

The financial criteria widely used by purchasers and experienced advisers alike are:

- An earnings-multiple approach
- Discounted cash flow analysis techniques
- Return on investment
- Impact on earnings per share for a listed company making an acquisition
- Net asset backing
- Valuation rules of thumb in the sector

The less easily quantified factors which should be taken into account include:

- Strategic significance or rarity value
- A defensive need to acquire
- Cost rationalisation opportunities

Each of the above criteria and factors will be explored in detail.

Earnings multiples

An earnings-multiple approach to the valuation of a business means that the purchase price is calculated by:

- taking the adjusted profit before tax for the previous financial year
- deducting a full tax charge, calculated at the standard corporation tax rate
- multiplying the above profit after tax by an appropriate number of years

The application of this method depends upon the appropriate number of years chosen to multiply the profits after tax, which are often referred to as earnings.

The basis of this method is an attempt to relate the value of unquoted companies to similar companies listed on a stock market in the same country. Stock market listed companies have a price earnings ratio, often described as a PE ratio, which is the equivalent of an earnings multiple.

A PE Ratio is calculated as follows:

$$\text{PE Ratio} = \frac{\text{present market share price}}{\text{historical earnings per share}}$$

This historical earnings per share is the profits after tax for the previous financial year, divided by the average number of issued shares during that year.

An illustration may be helpful. Assume:

present market share price	= 182p
previous year's profit after tax	= £26.0 million
average number of issued shares that year	= 200.0 million
therefore, earnings per share	$= \dfrac{£26.0}{200.0}$ = 13p
therefore, PE Ratio	$= \dfrac{182p}{13p}$ = 14.0

It is accurate to state as a generalisation, however, that an unquoted company would be valued at a lower earnings multiple than the PE Ratio which exists for a listed company carrying out a similar business in the same market sector.

A major reason for this difference can be explained by the fact that there is not a market, and hence no opportunity to buy and sell shares, in the equity of an unquoted company. In the case of a private company, the success of the business may be unduly dependent upon the continued executive involvement and commitment of the present owners during the short to medium-term. This will therefore, tend to reduce the worth of the business to a prospective purchaser.

Recent empirical evidence shows that the earning multiples reflected in the prices paid for unquoted companies reveal discounts ranging from 30 to 40 percent compared to the PE Ratio of a quoted company in the same market sector with similar prospects for the rate of future profit growth. The size of the discount is influenced by the attractiveness of a market sector in terms of future growth and the availability of companies to acquire.

If the company to be sold is suitable to obtain a stock market quotation, and it is ready to float quickly, then a value of the business should be negotiated on the basis of the PE Ratio which would apply on flotation, less the total costs of admission to the stock market. Any suggestion of a discount on the comparable PE Ratio should therefore be rejected.

The shortcomings of earnings multiples to value an unquoted business are:

- the after tax profit used is the previous years figure, because this is the basis for calculating PE Ratios, and does not reflect current or anticipated future performance which are fundamental for valuing a business.

- the number of years chosen to use as a multiplier is necessarily subjective.

- the method does not reflect strategic significance, rarity value, brand strength or major cost rationalisation opportunities.

None the less, earnings multiples do provide a useful guide to vendors.

Private equity houses often use a different version of earnings multiples for valuation, known as EBITDA multiples. EBITDA stands for:

- Earnings
- Before
- Interest
- Corporation Tax
- Depreciation and
- Amortization

Not only is the earnings figure used before tax, but it is before interest because private equity houses often buy companies free of cash and debt. Also, depreciation and amortization charges are ignored because these are accounting charges to the profit and loss account, rather than cash payments from the business. So, EBITDA is regarded as a rough guide to the operating cash flow generated by a business. As tax, depreciation and amortization are excluded, however, the multiples used are invariably lower.

Discounted cash flow analysis techniques

Whole books have been devoted to the application of discounted cash flow analysis techniques, so it will be appreciated that only an outline of the method can be given here.

Discounted cash flow techniques are widely used by sizeable companies for the evaluation of capital expenditure projects. The technique requires the cash flows to be calculated over a period of several years. Therefore, the cash flow elements which need to be quantified, for valuing a company are:

- the initial purchase consideration;
- subsequent earn-out payments;
- the annual operating cash flow from the business taking into account all capital expenditure needs and movements in working capital;
- the realisable value of the assets remaining at the end of the period chosen for the evaluation; and
- taxation payments.

The discounted cash flow process can be used to evaluate the pattern of cash outflows and inflows to produce different measures of performance. These are:

NET PRESENT VALUE

This is sometimes referred to as NPV, and is the present value of the cash flows calculated at the percentage discount rate set by the company. Provided that the NPV is a positive figure, rather than a negative one, it means that the acquisition is calculated to exceed the rate of return required by the company.

INTERNAL RATE OF RETURN OR % DCF RATE OF RETURN

The rate of return calculation is much more widely used than net present values. The rate of return is found by calculating the discount rate at which the net present value of the cash outflows and inflows equals zero over the evaluation period chosen.

DISCOUNTED PAY BACK PERIOD

The discounted pay back period is the number of years required to generate sufficient cash, discounted usually at a standard rate of 10 per cent, to equal or 'pay back' the initial cash outflow.

Whereas it is not unusual for companies to expect or demand a discounted pay back period not exceeding three years for organic growth projects, the premiums over net asset value paid to acquire companies means that the periods may be considerably longer for acquisition.

Discounted cash flow analysis is extremely relevant conceptually for the evaluation of acquisitions because it focuses entirely on the generation of cash. There are some pitfalls, however, when using the method and it is important to be aware of these.

Companies use lengthy periods for evaluation, ranging from five or seven years to as long as fifteen or twenty years. Obviously, the accuracy of the cash flow projections after the first two or three years must be questionable. Fortunately, the weighting given to cash flows in later years is much less than for the early years because this is inherent in the nature of the calculations.

With a large group, it is desirable to set a standard number of years over which any acquisition will be evaluated to ensure uniformity of evaluation.

One other subjective issue is the realisable value of the assets remaining at the end of the period of evaluation. When using discounted cash flow techniques to evaluate internal capital expenditure projects, it is usual merely to include the market value of land and buildings and whatever value might be realised for other assets. For consistency of treatment, most companies tend to use a similar approach for acquisition evaluation. This means they do not assume that the business will be sold as a going concern, at a premium over net asset value, at the end of the period. On the other hand, private equity investors will include the likely exist value from the sale or listing of the company because an exit is paramount.

One of the real benefits of using discounted cash flow techniques is the use of sensitivity analysis to answer 'what if' questions. For example, an advertising agency acquiring a competitor might rightly be concerned at the risk of losing a major account because of a conflict of interest caused by representing two clients in the same business sector. Sensitivity analysis allows another percentage rate of return and discounted pay back period calculation to be made quickly to determine the effect of the loss of a client.

In summary, discounted cash flow techniques are used by some of the more sophisticated acquirers. Even if the discounting is not done, the calculation of annual cash flows alone will give a valuable insight into the benefits to be gained by the acquirer.

Return on investment

By now, readers who are not accountants may be wishing that a simple rule of thumb could be provided.

Well it can. The return on investment is easily calculated. What is more, this simple method is popular with group chief executives of large companies as a way to cut through the complicated financial analysis, often carried out by their corporate finance staff.

Return on investment, often abbreviated as ROI, can be defined in various ways. A simple and useful definition is:

$$\text{percentage return on investment} = \frac{\text{pre-tax profit from acquisition}}{\text{cash invested}}$$

A simplified example may be helpful. Consider a facilities management contracting firm purchased for £4.8 million and earn-out payments of £0.6 million expected to be paid in each of the next two years. Further information is set out below:

	Current Year	Next Year	Second Full Year
Pre-tax profit forecast	£0.7M	£0.8M	£1.0M
Purchase consideration	£(4.8)M	£(0.6)M	£(0.6)M
Net cash generated from operations	£0.2M	£0.8M	£0.4M
Cumulative net cash outlay	£4.6M	£4.8M	£4.6M
Return on investment =	£0.7M / £4.6M = 15.2%	£0.8M / £4.8M = 16.7%	£1.0M / £4.6M = 21.7%

Most companies seek to achieve a return of between 15 and 25 percent on the above basis by the end of the second year following acquisition.

Net asset backing

For a company achieving reasonable profitability, net asset backing will be a secondary factor in determining the price to be paid. In a service company where asset backing is particularly low, such as a firm of insurance brokers, the impact is likely to be an insistence on an earn-out deal.

When a company is making losses or doing only a little better than breaking-even, asset backing is likely to have an important effect on the purchase price.

With a loss-making company, the purchase value is likely to be significantly less than the net asset value at the time of negotiating the purchase. Assume the company is making losses at the rate of £500,000 a year, and there will be an interval of, say, six weeks between negotiation and legal completion. This means that the net worth will have diminished by about £60,000 in the meantime, because the losses are roughly £10,000 per week. Furthermore, it is likely to take months rather than weeks to eliminate losses after legal completion, which will further diminish the net asset worth before profits are achieved. Also, it has to be said that purchasers are likely to attach only a minimal value to accumulated tax losses to be carried forward.

When selling a loss-making company, the reality often becomes horse-trading to negotiate the discount on net asset value rather than carrying out a valuation. A forecast of dramatic profit growth within the next two or three years, despite losses in the previous and current years, will be viewed cautiously by prospective purchasers. Their likely reaction is to offer an initial payment related to present net asset worth, and earn-out payments for the achievement of worthwhile profits in the future.

So the message is clear. Take urgent action to restore profits in loss-making companies before selling them. The impact on the purchase price is likely to be substantial. Yet all too often, groups choose to sell a subsidiary because it is making a loss. This is the worst possible time to sell. What is more, the only purchaser may be the management team wishing to pursue a buy-out and so reap the benefits for themselves.

Turning round loss-making companies prior to sale is so important that Chapter 10 is devoted to how to do it!

Impact on earnings per share

Companies listed on a stock market are keen to ensure that significant earnings per share growth is achieved every year.

Earnings per share are the profits after tax earned for the benefit of ordinary shareholders divided by the number of issued shares.

This has two effects on the price a particular listed company is likely to be prepared to pay for acquisitions.

Firstly, there is a psychological resistance for a listed company to pay a higher multiple for an unquoted company in the same sector than the PE Ratio of their own shares. This may seem illogical, and it can be argued so. None the less, it is often a reality. So it must be realised that a company with a low PE Ratio may offer a relatively low price.

Secondly, when the acquisition is significant relative to the size of a listed bidder, and it is being financed by a placing of shares or the issue of convertible loan stock, the company will wish to ensure that the acquisition will not adversely affect their earnings per share growth throughout the medium-term.

Valuation rules of thumb in the sector

In various market sectors, a rule of thumb for valuing a business may be widely accepted as an approximate guide. Quite often, these are not based on either profit or cash flow. Although some accountants may regard them as unscientific, rules of thumb should not be dismissed. Hotel valuations worldwide are often linked to a price per bedroom. In the UK, public houses are valued in terms of a price per barrel of beer and lager, applied to the annual volume of barrels sold. Software business valuations may be linked to turnover.

It is useful to find out what rule of thumb exists in your business sector, because it is surprising how often buyers will pay heed to it in order to avoid overpaying.

Strategic significance or rarity value

There is ample evidence that purchasers will pay more than a financial evaluation alone would dictate when there is strategic significance to be gained. For example, a media services group seeking to offer one-stop shopping to clients may have a strong qualitative market research arm but lack quantitative competence. If acquisition is the only way to gain this quickly enough, there may well be a willingness to pay a premium price.

A scarcity of acquisition targets becomes rarity when there is only one attractive company available to acquire in a country in a particular market segment. Recently, US medical and orthopaedic product companies have been keen to acquire in the UK and Ireland, but the lack of private companies which are suitable acquisition targets means that scarcity is rapidly becoming rarity value. In such a situation, competitive bidding may deliver an outstanding deal for vendors.

Defensive need to acquire

The defensive need to acquire may arise when a private company creates a new product, service or distribution network which is likely to threaten the existing business of a major company.

In these circumstances, the company under threat is likely to take into account not only the additional profit resulting from the acquisition of the private company, but also the loss of existing profits if the competitor is allowed to continue. Once again, the advantage may prove to be only temporary, so the timing of the sale is important.

Sometimes, stock market listed companies feel themselves to be under pressure to make an acquisition, either to diversify into more attractive market sectors or to reduce their own vulnerability to acquisition. If they believe this to be the case, whether it is a correct analysis or not, it is likely to encourage them to pay a somewhat more generous price as a result.

Cost rationalisation opportunities

Some acquisitions produce substantial cost rationalisation opportunities for the purchaser. Consider a private contract caterer which operates in a local geographic area and enjoys a high market share. A nationwide acquirer would be able to virtually eliminate the directors, head office staff and costs by folding the business under the existing regional management structure. Consequently, the rule of thumb in the market sector is to value businesses on a multiple of gross profit. In these circumstances, it is unlikely that an overseas acquirer wishing to enter the market could match the price because there would not be similar overhead savings.

The approach to valuation

By now it will be realised that there is much more to valuation than the use of formulae and yardsticks. None the less, rigorous financial analysis is the foundation, to which should be added insight and judgement. What is more, several methods of calculation should be used. It is definitely inadvisable to choose one favourite method of valuation, thereby rejecting other techniques.

Another vital point to emphasis is that the value placed on a given business is likely to be different from one prospective purchaser to the next. The particular valuation will depend on the ability to pay and the incremental benefits to be gained.

Executive summary

- Individual vendors of private companies should assess whether the net capital sum to be received will allow early retirement and their present lifestyle to be maintained.

- Fundamental valuation factors are the incremental profits and cash flow to be gained by each prospective purchaser, and to a lesser extent, the worth of the assets acquired.

- Adjusted profits, cash flows and balance sheets should be used for valuation calculations.

- Several financial criteria should be used, including:
  - earnings multiples
  - discounted cash flow techniques
  - return on investment
  - valuation rules of thumb in the sector
  - net asset backing, for a loss-making company

- Less quantifiable factors which affect prices include:
  - scarcity and rarity value
  - cost rationalisation opportunities for the acquirer

SEVEN
How to find and handle prospective purchasers

To avoid a waste of management time and the risk of damaging the business, once a valuation of the worth of the company has been made, the next steps should be:

- to confirm the decision to sell; and

- to set the minimum price acceptable.

In the light of the valuation, it may make sense to delay the sale until either losses have been eliminated or current profits have been increased, in order to achieve an acceptable price.

What may be less obvious is the importance of setting the minimum acceptable price. A decision to sell a business needs to be based on a minimum price in order to be meaningful. If professional advisers think it is unlikely that the minimum acceptable price required will be obtainable, then the right decision may well be to improve the profitability of the business before selling it. To seek different professional advisers may be wrong. Some will glibly talk about an attractive price simply to win the assignment. The important thing is to find out the reasons and evidence for any views on valuation put forward by professional advisers.

Find first, contact later

A pitfall to avoid is approaching one or two prospective purchasers, perhaps chosen because of suitable personal contacts, reaching the point of final negotiation, and then involving professional advisers. They may believe that other purchasers would offer a significantly better price, but by then it will be too late to avoid the risk of losing the present deal.

The clear message is:

- identify all prospective purchasers first, from both home and overseas;
- decide the method of approach; and
- work to a timetable.

Each of these steps will be considered in turn.

Identify prospective purchasers

It is essential to identify all likely purchasers at home and overseas, or in a few cases, decide that it is almost impossible to do so because of the small size and nature of the business.

Overseas purchasers are potentially attractive because there is definite evidence that companies do tend to pay higher prices when acquiring abroad. One possible reason is that it is more difficult to identify and handle acquisitions overseas, because of the management time required and the extra costs involved, so when an opportunity is found there is an extra determination to do a deal.

An actual example illustrates the improbability in a few cases of identifying prospective purchasers. The company in question sold Christmas gift hampers by mail order and made a profit before tax in excess of £100,000 a year. It was managed entirely by the owner, with the support of low-grade and mostly temporary staff. An important feature of the product was the supply of attractive merchandise obtained direct from specialist suppliers in several countries. As a result of terminal illness, an urgent sale of the business was essential.

It was decided that companies already in the hamper market may be unwilling to pay an attractive price. The view was taken that a private individual or company may be a more likely buyer, and that in this case an advertisement would be needed to reach the widest number of potential buyers.

The more usual ways of identifying prospective purchasers include:

- personal contacts;
- business brokers;
- registers; and
- specific research.

Each of these will be considered separately.

PERSONAL CONTACTS

The directors of the company to be sold will be able to identify some prospective purchasers, such as:

- previous approaches to buy the business which were rejected;
- competitors;
- major customers or suppliers, but often these prove to be unlikely purchasers; and
- companies which are complementary.

An example of a complementary company is one which sells to the same customers or through the same distribution channels. A bathroom fitting importer, selling to do-it-yourself retail chains, may be attracted to a company selling home security products through the same outlets.

Perhaps the most difficult source of prospective purchasers to be identified from within the company are overseas buyers, simply because of a possible lack of involvement with them as customers, suppliers or competitors.

BUSINESS BROKERS

Business brokers may seem an ideal choice. After all, their prime job is the introduction of buyers and sellers to each other. It must be remembered, however, that their 'no deal – no fee' basis of reward means they are motivated to complete deals and not necessarily to secure the best possible price, or to be concerned about who is the purchaser. The deal is the thing for them, and they are paid by the purchaser.

Another factor to be considered is confidentiality. Some brokers are always ready to talk about possible deals, even gossip about them, to produce results. They may have reciprocal arrangements with other brokers to share fees when a sale results from an introduction by another broker.

So, before appointing a business broker, obtain satisfactory answers to the following questions:

- Will the identity of the company for sale be revealed only to prospective purchasers with my specific approval?

- Is the broker retained by any companies, or does the broker know of others, looking to acquire a similar business?

- What specific research will be done to identify other purchasers at home and overseas?

- How will the broker contact prospective purchasers, and screen them before a meeting with the vendors?

- Who are three recent vendors willing to be telephoned as satisfied clients?

Some brokers pursue potential vendors aggressively. If they are not appointed immediately to handle the sale, they may seek to introduce prospective purchasers anyway to win the assignment or pull off a deal, even if another company has been appointed as advisers.

REGISTERS

Banks, stockbrokers, chartered accountants, acquisition and disposal specialists and business brokers, are amongst those who maintain registers of the requirements of acquirers and companies for sale. Usually, these are strictly confidential and remain unpublished.

A comprehensive list of buyers' requirements is useful. It may allow one or more prospective buyers to be identified immediately. An important feature is a register which includes the diversification plans of major companies. Otherwise, it may not be realised that a bookseller wishes to diversify into commercial stationery supply, or whatever. Importantly, companies eager to diversify into a specific sector may be ready to pay an attractive price.

None the less, it has to be said that a register should be regarded only as a valuable database to be used to complement specific research to locate prospective purchasers. Evidence shows that reliance on a register alone is unlikely to produce the best possible deal.

Whilst an acquisition register may be helpful, vendors should be reluctant to join a disposal register. These are maintained by business brokers and some firms of chartered accountants. Companies tend to be small, unattractive for some reason or loss-making, which means that advisers are unwilling to spend effort marketing them. Acquirers tend to view disposal registers with suspicion, asking themselves what is wrong with the company to be put on a disposal register. An attractive and saleable company should be discreetly marketed and not left to languish on a disposal register.

SPECIFIC RESEARCH

There is no substitute for specific research to identify as many prospective purchasers as possible from home and overseas. In the recent sale of a UK based niche pet-food manufacturer, interested purchasers included companies from mainland Europe, the USA and one in Australia.

It tends to be corporate finance specialists who have the experience and resources to carry out this specific research. Before appointing one, as there will be a fee involved to demonstrate a commitment to sell, be satisfied that they have a proven competence, and will be able to handle each stage of the transaction through to legal completion.

Methods of approach

Having identified prospective purchasers, the possible methods of approach include:

- a direct approach;
- advertisement;
- press release; and
- auction.

In some cases, more than one avenue of approach will be used, but it is helpful to consider each separately.

DIRECT APPROACH

It is not unusual for specific research to identify between ten and twenty possible purchasers, and occasionally even more. The next step needs to be a grouping or classification, under categories such as:

- short-list;
- reserve list; and
- others.

In order to maintain confidentiality, one or more competitors may be deliberately excluded from the short-list and possibly kept on the reserve list.

The research work should identify the name of the individual to be contacted in each company. In a major multi-national, it is more likely to be the person in charge of a relevant subsidiary or a group business development executive, rather than the corporate chief executive officer.

The telephone is a more effective and flexible means of direct approach than a letter. If the specialist advisers are also involved in helping companies to achieve a flotation on a stock market and providing initial strategic advice, it allows a possible sale to be portrayed accurately as one of the options being considered.

The purpose of the telephone conversation should simply be to establish an interest to purchase a similar company without disclosing the identity of the vendors. The next step would be to have a confidentiality agreement signed by the prospective purchaser. The confidentiality agreement should:

- bind the professional advisers to the purchaser;

- preclude any disclosure of information or indication of the possibility of a sale to a third party;

- specifically prohibit poaching staff for a set period using knowledge gained; and

- require the return of all documents provided, and any copies taken, unless the purchase is completed.

None the less, a competitor can gain commercially valuable information merely by pursuing a possible acquisition.

Using the direct approach, it is desirable not to have more than about five interested parties in order to be manageable 'in parallel' by the vendors, and to maintain as much confidentiality as possible.

PRESS ADVERTISEMENT

If it has been decided that specific research is unlikely to identify prospective purchasers, then press advertising should be considered, rather than relying on a register.

A decision needs to be made whether to advertise in a newspaper or a trade magazine. If the objective is to reach the widest possible spectrum of prospective purchasers, then a newspaper is probably more appropriate.

It is assumed that the identify of the company will not be disclosed. So the advert could be placed using a box number or in the name of an accountant, solicitor or specialist adviser.

To get the best possible response from an advert there are several features which should be included:

- a heading such as 'For Sale – Christmas Hamper Company', unless the advertisement is to be inserted in a Business for Sale column, so that the nature of the advertisement is obvious;

- a location, without being specific enough to reveal the identify of the company;

- sales turnover, expressed approximately;

- an indication of profitability, preferably profit before tax; and

- the name of the professional adviser handling replies and a contact telephone number to make it easy for people to respond to the advert.

Another avenue to consider when preparing an advert is to use the heading 'Christmas Hamper Company – Acquisition, Merger or Sale'. This establishes that a sale of the business is only one of the options being considered.

PRESS RELEASE

A large company intending to sell a sizeable subsidiary or division may decide to issue a press release to the national and trade press announcing the disposal. This assumes that a definite decision to sell has been made, there will be several interested buyers likely to pay an acceptable price and the people working in the business have been informed.

The press release – or press conference, if the disposal is sufficiently news-worthy – may include comments such as:

- A certain target price is expected

- An alternative being considered is a separate flotation of the business

- The disposal is being handled by a particular bank or specialist adviser so purchasers know who to contact

- An auction will be carried out, the deadline for the receipt of initial offers, and the sale is expected to be completed within a stated period

Work to a timetable

Whilst a business is being sold, a state of limbo may exist. There is an understandable tendency to defer important capital expenditure, management recruitment and discretionary revenue items, such as an expensive website upgrade. Also, the longer the sale process is allowed to take, the greater is the risk of rumour and speculation amongst staff, customers and suppliers. So a realistic timetable should be set and adhered to.

Some banks and specialist advisers have demonstrated an ability to dispose of businesses by auction. An important feature of an auction is that a timetable is usually decided upon at the outset. In contrast, when a business is sold by direct approaches to prospective buyers there is often a tendency for events to drift. This is unacceptable, and should not be allowed to happen.

The auction and direct approach methods will be outlined in turn.

SALE BY AUCTION

The auction method is being used more widely, but is largely restricted to the disposal of subsidiaries and divisions by groups.

The approach is to notify all prospective purchasers simultaneously that a disposal is to be made. Whilst a press release to both the national and trade press should notify all prospective purchasers in the particular country, it has to be assumed that this will not achieve sufficient coverage overseas. So, prospective purchasers overseas should be researched and approached direct at the same time. Alternatively, if it is considered that any press coverage would be undesirable, a direct approach should be made to companies at home as well as overseas.

Some auctions will produce more than twenty replies, and the aim should be quickly to reduce this number to two or three companies for serious negotiation.

The stages and timescales involved may be as follows:

Timescale	Stage
Week 1	Confidentiality agreements signed and detailed Memorandum of Sale despatched to principals and their advisers.
Week 5	Outline written offers to be received.
Week 7	Up to about five prospective purchasers short-listed.
Weeks 8 to 10	Each short-listed company allowed to meet the management team and given access to a data room containing detailed information about the business.
Week 12	Outline written offers confirmed or amended.
Week 14	Detailed negotiations with up to three prospective purchasers completed. Final due diligence and legal contract negotiations commence.

To accelerate legal completion, the vendors may prepare and present the purchase contract to be signed. Normally, of course, it is the lawyers to the purchaser who prepare the purchase contract. Dependent upon the size and method of financing the purchase, however, further time may be required to obtain stock exchange approval or shareholder agreement by the purchaser.

An important benefit of an auction is that a significantly higher price may be obtained.

SALE BY DIRECT APPROACH

The aim should be to approach sufficient prospective purchasers simultaneously so that up to six companies have an initial meeting with the vendors, after a preliminary screening meeting with the specialist advisers.

An outline of the stages and timescale required is:

Timescale	Stage
Week 1	Prospective purchasers telephoned to establish up to six seriously interested companies, and confidentiality agreements signed.
Weeks 2 and 4	Outline description of business provided and preliminary screening meetings with advisers if appropriate.
Weeks 5 and 6	Preliminary meetings with vendors.
Weeks 7 and 8	Supplementary information provided to acceptable purchasers.
Week 10	Written offers received.
Week 12	Preferred purchaser selected. Detailed negotiations completed and Heads of Agreement signed.

Clearly, at least one other interested purchaser should be kept in reserve. It is unrealistic, however, to think that the detailed negotiations required to produce Heads of Agreement can take place with several purchasers.

Memorandum for sale

If the business is to be auctioned a comprehensive Memorandum for Sale is required. This has to contain sufficient information to enable prospective purchasers to make a meaningful outline written offer, without visiting the premises or meeting the management.

Usually, the Memorandum for Sale will be written by the advisers to the company, based on information supplied to them by the management. The contents will need to include:

- an executive summary;
- a description of the business;
- a history;
- present and previous ownership;
- market segments and countries served;
- products and services;
- manufacture or sources of supply;
- major customers and distribution channels;
- location and premises;
- management and staff;
- intellectual property;
- reason for sale; and
- financial information.

The financial information will need to include:

- profit and loss accounts for the previous three years;
- current year budget and latest year end forecast;
- future years' projections;
- details of all intra-group charges;
- cash flow projections;
- latest balance sheet;

- schedule of key assets; and

- statement of accounting policies.

It must be remembered that the Memorandum for Sale should be a selling document as well. Future benefits and opportunities should be outlined.

Information memorandum

When a business is to be sold by a direct approach to prospective purchasers, the cost and time required to write a detailed and lengthy Memorandum for Sale should be avoided.

None the less, it is important to give an Information Memorandum to each prospective purchaser after a confidentiality agreement has been signed, to ensure uniformity of information.

The content of an Information Memorandum should be broadly similar to a Memorandum for Sale, but limited to no more than 12 to 15 pages of narrative, plus an appendix setting out profit and loss history, current year forecast and future projections, together with the latest available balance sheet.

The Information Memorandum needs to be written as a sales document, emphasising the opportunities available to a new owner which the vendors may not have pursued. Commercially sensitive information should be omitted, however, and provided only to selected purchasers when necessary.

Giving an asking price

Don't! It is trite but true that a vendor who gives an asking price will never achieve it, let alone do better, regardless of how it is phrased. An asking price, or willingness to give one when asked, is evidence that the vendors are ready or even committed to sell.

It is much better to adopt an ambiguous stance. For example:

> *"we have received a couple of unsolicited approaches recently, and although we had not thought about selling, we have decided to invite a small number of carefully selected companies to make an offer, but unless we receive a really attractive offer, we will continue to own and develop the company as we always intended."*

The subject of purchase price should be raised with prospective purchasers at the first meeting, at least in broad terms. Each purchaser should be asked to outline their basis for valuation, and either indicate a likely deal value or at least disclose the valuation used in recent deals they have completed. If their valuation appears unacceptable, then this should have a bearing on how the talks are to be progressed, or not. There is no reason to provide supplementary information unless the likely deal value is acceptable.

Some corporate finance advisers insist that prospective purchasers make a written indicative offer in order to be selected for an initial meeting with the vendors, but this could become a meaningless game. Prospective purchasers may well make a temptingly high offer, probably expressed as a broad range, simply to ensure a meeting with the vendors. Some serious bidders may be more honest, and not be selected, whilst some overseas purchasers simply may not be prepared to make a 'blind' indicative offer for an overseas target company.

When an indicative offer is made face to face, the vendors must be controlled and measured. Even if an unexpectedly higher offer is made, even a hint of a smile would be unthinkable. The reaction must always be that a better offer was expected. If pressed to respond by giving an asking price, there is no obligation whatsoever to give a figure. An answer saying we need time to think about it might be the most appropriate answer.

Handling purchaser visits

Visits to company premises by prospective purchasers should be kept to an absolute minimum to minimise rumour and speculation, and if necessary take place outside of normal working hours.

The initial meeting between vendor and purchaser should not take place on the company premises.

The scope of the first meeting should be to:

- Find out about the prospective purchaser, and their method of making acquisitions and managing them afterwards.

- Obtain details of any relevant acquisitions they have made during the previous three years, together with prices paid and basis of valuation.

- Find out what thoughts they have about developing the company under their ownership, including relocation or headcount reduction as a result of rationalisation.

- Outline the benefits, opportunities and potential of the business for them.

- Avoid giving commercially sensitive information at this stage.

If a decision to pursue matters is to be taken, then a visit to the premises will be required. None the less, it should be carefully controlled.

The visit to company premises should be restricted to seeing the facilities. The provision of detailed information can take place equally as well in a nearby hotel, provided adequate notice is given of what is desired. Furthermore, there may be departments such as research and development where it would be inappropriate to provide access until after a detailed verbal agreement for the sale has been reached, or Heads of Agreement signed.

During the brief visit to the premises any conversation and discussion should be restricted only to those people who are directly involved in the sale of the business.

There may be detailed information requested which is commercially sensitive and this should only be given when oral negotiations have been completed. When dealing with a competitor, this issue becomes more important still.

Information which may be commercially sensitive includes:

- specific details about the mix of business, volumes, prices and discounts with major customers;

- process know-how, especially where patent protection does not exist;

- details of new product development or research projects; and

- sources of supply from overseas, where no exclusive supply agreement exists.

External accountants should not be allowed to carry out an on-site investigation until detailed oral negotiations have been completed, Heads of Agreement signed and a draft purchase contract has been received. Yet vendors sometimes allow it to happen. Specialist advisers would not. It is difficult to avoid rumour, speculation and probably the knowledge that the business is to be sold during an accountancy investigation, even though a 'cover story' may have been given to explain people visiting the premises for several days.

Executive summary

- Identify all likely purchasers from home and overseas using specific research, before contacting any of them.

- Evidence shows that overseas purchasers are likely to pay higher prices.

- If a business broker is to be used, insist on telephoning two or three recent clients before appointing them.

- Avoid placing your business on a Disposal Register, because many of the companies are loss making or unattractive ones.

- The telephone is an effective way of your corporate finance adviser making a direct approach to a prospective purchaser, without revealing the identify of the business.

- An auction can be an effective method of selling a subsidiary or division of a group, based on a comprehensive Memorandum for Sale.

- The sale of a private company should be carried out within a broad timetable, and it is important to prepare an Information Memorandum of the business for prospective purchasers.

- The question of purchase price should be raised in broad terms at the first meeting, without disclosing an asking price.

- Visits to the company premises should be kept to a minimum.

EIGHT
How to negotiate a deal

Negotiation is an art not a science. Furthermore, negotiating the sale of a business is deceptively complex. It requires an awareness of the relevant taxation and legal regulations in the country concerned. Otherwise, unknowingly, a seemingly attractive deal may be negotiated, with onerous tax consequences or unacceptable legal implications.

Earn-out deals add another level of complexity. Some people mistakenly think that the drafting of the earn-out formulae can be safely left to experienced lawyers. It can, but only if the commercial details have been resolved between the purchasers and vendors first.

Emotional involvement is a problem for the vendors of a private company. The degree of personal turmoil is comparable to an acrimonious divorce. An unacceptably low offer or a critical comment about the company may well be treated as a personal insult. People selling a business for a multinational group may be equally lacking in previous experience of negotiating acquisitions and disposals. They may be senior executives, but still come off second best against expert professional advisers.

Countless vendors of private companies have said words to the effect that 'I never want to go through an experience like that again'. In one case, when the purchaser withdrew for seemingly inadequate reasons less than a week before legal completion, the owner said 'it will be several years before I can face selling the company again'.

If negotiations are about to take place, and professional advisers have not been appointed, the unequivocal advice is to consider appointing them immediately.

There are three key features for negotiating the sale of a business successfully:

1. establishing the deal format

2. negotiating the price and other features

3. agreeing the forms of purchase consideration

Each of these will be considered separately.

The deal format

Two extremes are to be avoided in negotiating the sale of a business. Firstly, negotiations which are spread out over several months with one purchaser. This is quite unnecessary and unacceptable. Secondly, being persuaded into ('hustled into' is a more accurate phrase) commencing and completing negotiations in a single meeting.

A two stage approach is strongly recommended:

- An initial meeting to agree a deal format and, subject to satisfactory agreement, to set a date for; and

- a detailed negotiation meeting to agree the price and key features so that Heads of Agreement can be written and signed, and lawyers can be instructed to draft the share purchase and sale agreement.

Key elements of the format for a deal include:

- What is to be sold

- Outright sale or earn-out deal

- The price range

- Purchase of assets

- Key considerations

- Management continuity

- Profit warranties

Each of these will be considered in turn.

What is to be sold

The purchaser may suggest that the assets and intellectual property are sold rather than the share capital of the company. This has the attraction for the purchaser that any skeletons in the cupboard are safely left behind. From the vendor's viewpoint, a sale of assets may be less attractive because of taxation problems.

If the assets of a private company are sold rather than the equity, only a shell will remain containing the proceeds of the sale. The purchasers will insist, however, that the name of the company is transferred to them and that the vendors cease trading immediately. So in the UK and some countries there will be extra tax payable to extract the proceeds of the sale from the company for the benefit of the individual shareholders.

Whenever a group intends to dispose of the assets and intellectual property of a business, expert advice should be taken before the decision is made to ensure that tax liabilities are minimised.

If some property is owned by individual shareholders, and used by the business, they may prefer to grant only a medium-term lease in order to retain the development potential which exists from the possibility of obtaining permission for alternative use, or because of future road construction which will increase the value of the site.

A particular subsidiary or part of the business may not be of interest or attractive to the purchaser. The vendors should not overlook the opportunity to exclude it from the sale, with little impact on the purchase price to be obtained, and then either to retain it for themselves or to sell it at an attractive price separately. In an actual case, a business consisted of a chain of retail travel agents and a small but specialised inclusive tour operator. The purchaser only wanted the travel agency and was so keen to avoid the problems of managing a tour operator that it was agreed to exclude it at the deal format stage for a nominal sum. Two years later the tour operator was sold for a handsome price.

It may be necessary for a group selling a subsidiary to retain intellectual property rights, such as patents or brand names, for use elsewhere in the group and to grant a licence to the purchaser for particular use in certain countries.

Outright sale or earn-out deal

If the vendors expect an outright purchase this should have been said at the initial meeting with each prospective purchaser and should be confirmed at the meeting to discuss the deal format. It would be quite unacceptable to discover at the detailed negotiation stage that the only deal being offered is an earn-out one. Equally, it should be established that there will be no question of a retention of part of the purchase price for a given period after legal completion as a form of security for the warranties and indemnities to be given.

If an earn-out deal has been agreed in principle, then some of the features needing preliminary discussion are:

- The percentage of equity to be purchased initially – if less than 100 per cent, it is essential to ensure that the vendors will have the right to oblige the purchaser to buy the remainder within a given period valued on a formula set out in the legal contract in addition to the purchaser having similar rights. Expert tax advice is necessary to ensure that no additional capital gains tax liability will be crystallised immediately.

- The period of the earn-out – it can be argued that the shorter the earn-out period the better it is for vendors, and generally this will be true. Earn-out periods of longer than two years after the end of the current financial year should be strongly resisted. Longer than two more years may turn out to seem like a life sentence, and the likelihood of unforeseeable external factors which depress profits increases significantly beyond this period.

- The proportion of earn-out payments – in extreme cases earn-out deals have been completed where more than 90 per cent of the total purchase price has been dependent upon future performance. In contrast, some deals have earn-out payments of less than 10 per cent. With this range of possibilities, it is essential to discuss the proportion of earn-out payments which will apply.

Some purchasers propose an initial payment on an earn-out deal of less than the present net asset worth of the company. If the company is profitable, this should be categorically rejected. The aim should be to get an initial payment which fully reflects the worth of the business today. The earn-out payments should reflect an additional bonus for further profit achievement.

Price range

At the deal format stage, the aim is not necessarily to negotiate a specific purchase price but to confirm a narrow price range. Unless the low point of the range is acceptable, there is no point in arranging a detailed negotiation meeting.

Purchase of assets

Sometimes in the sale of a private company, the vendors will either wish, or be asked by the purchaser, to buy certain assets which are not really needed for the running of the business. Boats, aeroplanes and expensive motor cars may come into this category and should present no problem.

Occasionally something more unusual is involved. In one situation, a private company purchased a piece of land at the back of the site because it gave important access to land owned by the shareholders, and more importantly, they could not afford to buy it as individuals at the time. On this occasion, it was important to establish that the land would be excluded from the sale of the company, in order to retain the access.

Key conditions

It would be entirely wrong to get into detailed discussion about warranties and indemnities at the deal format stage. None the less, it is desirable to establish whether the purchaser is seeking any conditions which may be regarded as onerous, because it could be that these are totally unacceptable.

An example of this was the demand made by a purchaser that during a three-year earn-out period, earlier payments could be clawed back if subsequent profit thresholds were not achieved. To compound matters, the repayment was to include not only the original amount earned, but an interest penalty as well. Some plain speaking was needed to establish that such a condition was so unacceptable that it would become an immediate 'deal breaker' if pursued.

Management continuity

When payment is in full on legal completion, if the vendors wish to retire then the aim should be to agree the shortest reasonable period of continuity.

If one or more of the vendors is seeking a career with the larger group, then this should be discussed and a period for an initial service contract agreed, although the notice period will be in line with company policy.

Profit warranties

This may be the final point raised by the purchasers, and it carries a sting in the tail. The vendors may be asked to warrant pre-tax profits for the current financial year. If such a warranty is to be considered by the vendors, the first thing to be established is that there will be no financial penalty for failure to meet the warranted profit figure. In some cases, the penalty suggested has been as high as seven times the amount of the shortfall.

If profits are to be warranted, and the penalty for a shortfall is in any way onerous, then the figure warranted should be one that is easily achievable. Otherwise, instead of accepting a penalty for a shortfall, it is better for the vendors to seek an earn-out payment on any excess profit over the figure suggested for a warranty.

If the deal format meeting produces a satisfactory basis for valuation, then it makes sense to agree a date for the detailed negotiations. This should allow sufficient time for the vendors to be adequately prepared and advised. Equally, it is important to establish that the purchaser will have the requisite authority by that date. For example, the purchaser may be required to obtain formal approval from the main board to negotiate Heads of Agreement.

In a case involving a multinational electronics company, the vendors were badly treated in this respect. Detailed negotiations took place, a draft contract was sent to the vendors and the accountancy investigation commenced. Three weeks after the negotiations, the purchaser announced that the main board had instructed that the offer be reduced by 20 percent. Not surprisingly, the sale was never completed, but it was an unfortunate experience which is to be avoided.

Negotiating the deal

Detailed negotiations may require typically between three and twelve hours, sometimes longer. If much less than three hours is taken, there is a likelihood that some important issues have not been addressed.

It is desirable that the negotiations take place on neutral ground, perhaps in the offices of a professional adviser or in a hotel. A soundproof room, with a direct dial telephone, should be available for either side to adjourn.

A pre-negotiation meeting is strongly recommended. It ensures that everyone has assembled and is briefed on their role. A leader of the negotiation team should have been agreed upon.

Certain ground rules will have been established:

- No one will interrupt when a member of the other side is speaking, because a valuable point may be missed.

- When a question is asked of the other side, the person will be allowed to answer it in full.

- The negotiation team leader will interrupt one of his own team members if necessary.

- The temptation to become irritated or to score points will be resisted.

- The emphasis will be on listening.

Before the negotiating meeting, a draft agenda should be prepared. If the purchasers have prepared one as well, then the agenda for the meeting needs to be agreed at the outset. The agenda should be designed to ensure that all the issues needed to produce a meaningful agreement will be discussed and agreed.

A typical agenda could be:

- Update of events since last meeting

- Assets and business included in the sale

- Leases to be agreed

- Assets to be purchased by vendors

- Service contracts

- Consultancy agreements

- Retirement packages

- Earn-out deal structure

- Purchase price and consideration

- Timetable to legal completion

Some of these need to be considered separately.

Update of events

The opportunity must not be lost to confirm continued progress by the business since the last meeting. This could include:

- The latest set of monthly management accounts

- Sales figures for the month which has just ended

- Current month sales and orders received

- Important press coverage

- The successful launch of a new product or service

- A major new customer

Leases to be agreed

If freehold property is to be excluded from the sale, then the main provisions of a lease should be agreed. It is sufficient to agree the type of lease, the duration, the annual value and rent review dates. The remaining details should be left to the lawyers to draft.

Assets to be purchased by the vendors

The opportunity should be taken to obtain any assets to be purchased at an attractive price. As has been mentioned, these may include boats, aeroplanes, cars and surplus land or property.

Service contracts

The reality is that a group purchaser will be keen to ensure that salaries, motor cars and fringe benefits are in line with group policy. When someone is being asked to continue in full-time employment for a year or more after an outright sale, to provide management continuity, it is worth seeking to negotiate a profit-linked bonus for this period.

Consultancy agreement

Certain directors may wish to retire from full-time employment on legal completion, but can be available on an agreed basis for a given period. If so, the duration, duties, time to be spent, payment and expenses should be agreed so that a consultancy agreement can be prepared.

Retirement packages

The purchaser may require certain directors to leave immediately, even though they would prefer to continue. If so, it is worth pursuing a retirement package as compensation for loss of office. This requires a detailed knowledge of the taxation rules for the particular country.

Earn-out deals

Earn-out deals are a potential minefield for vendors. It is arguably more important to the purchaser, however, to produce an earn-out deal which works amicably in practice, because their aim should be to ensure the continued motivation of the vendors. None the less many purchasers, who should know better, enter into earn-out deals lacking in clarity which are likely to cause disagreement later.

The issues which need to be addressed include:

- initial payment;
- business development;
- finance costs;
- dividends;

- cost rationalisation;

- management charges;

- central service charges;

- intra-group trading;

- accounting policies;

- profit targets; and

- payment formula and limits.

Each of these needs to be considered separately.

INITIAL PAYMENT

The first thing to be agreed in any earn-out deal is the initial percentage of equity to be purchased, which usually will be 100 percent, and the amount to be paid. Unless this is acceptable, and reflects fully the value of the business today, there is no point in further discussion.

BUSINESS DEVELOPMENT

Vendors and purchasers alike need to outline their ideas for the development of the business during the earn-out period. The vendors will want to be satisfied that their plans for profitable expansion, and the finance required, are supported by the purchaser. In contrast, they will wish to learn about any diversification or overseas development plans the purchaser is keen to be pursued, if these could adversely affect profits during the earn-out period. If so, then it may be necessary to negotiate that these activities are accounted for separately and excluded from the earn-out calculations.

FINANCE COSTS

Many large groups electronically sweep clean the bank account of each subsidiary every evening, by transferring the balance to a group account. This means that the rate of interest to be credited on surplus funds generated and to be charged on borrowings must be agreed. Usually, this is expressed in terms of the number of percentage points difference from the bank rate at any time.

DIVIDENDS

Some groups levy a dividend charge on their subsidiaries, especially overseas ones. This needs to be quantified, because it will deplete cash resources and increase financing costs, so the profit thresholds should be reduced accordingly for earn-out purposes.

COST RATIONALISATION

It may be agreed that some cost rationalisation should take place after the sale, for example the closure of a branch or staff redundancy. If so, either an estimate of the cost needs to be agreed so that it can be included in the profit targets, along with the subsequent savings, or the costs should be borne by the purchasers.

MANAGEMENT CHARGES

The purchaser may require that matters such as legal services, payroll preparation and pension administration are handled centrally, and a charge levied for the service. More importantly, some groups levy a charge to subsidiaries reflecting the cost of certain central functions, such as research and development or publicity. These charges must be known before profit targets can be agreed for earn-out purposes and adjusted as necessary.

CENTRAL SERVICE CHARGES

The group may provide some services centrally which are charged on a usage basis. Examples include departments such as transport and website design. Clearly, the effect these charges will have on future profits must be assessed.

INTRA-GROUP TRADING

Some groups operate an entirely 'arms-length' basis of trading between subsidiaries, which means there is no obligation at all to trade with each other. When any trade is done, no preferential pricing is expected.

Other groups operate differently. They require that subsidiaries must trade with each other and have a transfer pricing policy. The company being sold may already do business with the group, and so the prices will be affected. Also, it may be required to buy from other group companies, at higher prices than could be obtained elsewhere. Once again, the profit impact of these arrangements must be assessed and the aim should be to negotiate that the group policy will not apply for earn-out purposes.

ACCOUNTING POLICIES

As soon as legal completion takes place, it must be assumed that group accounting policies will come into effect and the group auditors will be appointed. It should not be assumed, however, that earn-out payments must automatically be based on accounts prepared by group auditors using group accounting policies.

There is considerable merit in negotiating that, for the purposes of calculating earn-out payments, the vendors auditors will prepare the accounts using existing accounting policies, for review and approval by the group auditors. In this way, it is not necessary to assess the profit impact of different accounting policies, and any disagreement about their interpretation will be avoided.

PROFIT TARGETS

Before profit targets or thresholds are discussed, the amount expected to be earned in total should be agreed. Otherwise, there is a risk of agreeing to profit thresholds which are too high.

Purchasers are likely to want to set rising profit thresholds each year. Vendors should seek to negotiate a constant profit target based on the figure forecast for the current financial year. The crucial thing is that these figures take into account the profit effect of the factors outlined above.

PAYMENT FORMULA AND LIMITS

The understandable fear of any purchaser is that the vendors in an earn-out deal could adopt a wholly short-term approach in order to maximise the amount they receive. So a purchaser is likely to insist upon an upper limit on the earn-out payments. Provided this is sufficiently generous, the principle should be accepted.

The earn-out payment formula is likely to be based on a given multiple of the pre-tax profit in excess of a given figure. As well as seeking to increase the multiple, vendors should seek an additional lump sum for achieving the threshold figure each year, especially if the thresholds increase annually.

Purchase price and consideration

If the purchase is to be an earn-out deal, the price will have been agreed.

If it is an outright purchase, then this is the stage for the price to be agreed in the light of the agreement already reached on the other aspects of the sale outlined above.

It is at this stage that negotiation skills are of the essence. An attractive offer should be greeted with a sense of dismay. An adjournment will probably be requested. No visible attempt must be made to rush into an agreement.

Once the purchase price has been agreed the form of consideration needs to be discussed. It is important that vendors realise that the range of possible options includes:

- retirement packages;
- one-off pension contributions;
- advantageous purchase of assets;
- consultancy agreements; and
- purchase consideration.

Several of these items have already been covered. Whilst one-off lump-sum pension contributions may be tax effective, pension planning should have already occurred prior to the sale. What is more, vendors should add back excessive directors pension contributions when doing their adjusted profit calculations.

The forms of purchase consideration available require separate examination.

Purchase consideration

The consideration could be paid in various forms including:

- cash;
- unquoted shares; or
- quoted shares.

A decision to accept shares in an unquoted company requires careful consideration. By the time of legal completion, the purchaser will have subjected the business being bought to thorough scrutiny as a result of the due diligence carried out. In contrast, the vendors will have relatively little authoritative knowledge about the current situation and future prospects of the purchasing company. Their firm intention may be to sell a stock market quotation within one or two years, but unforeseeable events could delay this by several years. It has to be said that taking the purchase consideration in the shares of an unquoted company is a gamble.

Purchase consideration taken in shares of a quoted company is less of a gamble, but may still represent a significant risk. This applies particularly in the case of a smaller quoted company where the opportunity to sell a sizeable number of shares simply may not exist, because of the limited volume of dealing in the shares. Also, it means that the proceeds of the sale are invested in only one share, and it must make sense to spread the investment risk. When a significant amount of shares is to be received in a quoted company, the vendors are often asked to agree not to sell any shares for one or two years, and then only using the company stockbroker. A sale to institutional investors may need to be arranged whenever vendors wish to sell a large number of shares. In the space of less than a year, the shares of a quoted company may halve or double in value. This must not be overlooked.

Vendors are understandably keen to avoid or defer capital gains tax liability on the sale of their company. Shares in the purchasing company will defer any liability, but this does not remove the underlying risk.

Timetable to legal completion

Assuming that satisfactory agreement has been reached, the final stage of the meeting should be to agree an outline timetable culminating in the date of legal completion.

Vendors must realise that there is absolutely no cause whatsoever for celebration until legal completion takes place.

Some vendors selling to a management buy-out team have found the management deliberately delaying legal completion in an attempt to re-negotiate a better deal. Some vendors of private companies have found a quoted company delaying legal completion in order to issue a stock exchange circular covering another acquisition as well, particularly if some share placing with institutional investors is required to fund both purchases.

The detail of the timetable will be covered in the next chapter.

Overseas residency

Individual vendors who are to retire from the business immediately may wish to consider establishing overseas residency to avoid capital gains tax.

The fundamental point to be addressed is whether the shareholder and his or her family will be happy living abroad. A country may appear to offer an attractive lifestyle to a holidaymaker but the reality as a resident may be different. Language difficulties, medical needs, culture and lifestyle differences are some of the factors which must be considered carefully.

The other problem is taxation itself. In some countries such as the UK, the taxation rules require that overseas residency needs to be established before legal completion. Furthermore, a period of up to three years abroad may be advised to ensure tax problems are avoided later. One thing is certain: expert tax advice is needed long before legal completion.

Executive summary

- The negotiations to sell a business require a knowledge of the relevant taxation and legal rules in the country concerned.

- A two-stage approach is recommended:
    - establish the deal format in outline
    - negotiate the detailed agreement

- Key elements of the deal format include:
    - what is to be sold
    - essential features of an earn-out deal
    - price range
    - key conditions

- An agenda helps to ensure that all the issues are addressed at the detailed negotiation meeting.

- Some of the detailed features of an earn-out deal to be clarified are:
    - future development of the business
    - cost of finance
    - management charges
    - central service costs
    - intra-group pricing policy
    - accounting policies
    - profit targets and payment formula

- Possible forms of tax-effective purchase consideration may include:
    - retirement packages
    - lump-sum pension contributions
    - a pre-completion dividend to extra surplus cash
    - advantageous purchase of assets
    - shares and loan stock

NINE
How to handle legal completion

There is many a slip not only between cup and lip but also between verbal agreement and legal completion. This is a short chapter, but a vital one.

The first and important step towards legal completion should take place at the end of the verbal negotiation meeting, when the timetable to completion is agreed.

Timetable to completion

The timetable will usually include dates for:

- the signing of a heads of agreement or letter of intent, subject to contract;

- the receipt of the draft purchase contract from the acquirer;

- the commencement and completion of the accountancy and other due diligence investigation work to be done on site;

- the receipt of supplementary agreements such as service contracts;

- the receipt by the purchaser of the due diligence reports;

- a date reserved for a meeting with the principals and lawyers present to resolve any outstanding contractual matters;

- the receipt of the disclosure statement; and

- the legal completion and signing of documents.

This may seem somewhat hopeful, but slippage must be avoided. Realistic dates should be agreed, which people are committed to achieve. Accountants and lawyers must realise that they are working to strict deadlines. Vendors need to be acutely aware that the longer legal completion takes, the greater is the risk that some external event could wreck the deal. For example, the loss of a major client or a profit warning by the purchaser.

Each of the items will be considered separately.

Heads of agreement

Heads of agreement, sometimes referred to as a letter of intent, are not essential but are commonly used. At the least, however, it is important to have a written record of all the matters which have been agreed. This ensures a common understanding of what has been agreed, and serves to brief the lawyers.

Some purchasers, and some vendors too, like to make a little ceremony of the signing of heads of agreement. It should be recognised that:

- heads of agreement are usually non-binding, that is they are subject to contract and to satisfactory due diligence investigation;

- whilst it is useful to let a lawyer check the wording before signature, heads of agreement do not need to be written in the precise legal style of the purchase contract; and

- the purchaser will usually insist on a paragraph to preclude the vendor's having discussions with another prospective purchaser or announcing the proposed sale before the date of legal completion.

Draft purchase contract

The draft purchase contract will probably be at least forty pages long, and may exceed one hundred pages if a complex earn-out deal is involved.

Vendors should take the trouble to read the purchase contract, although it is likely to seem boring and unnecessarily pedantic. At the meeting with their lawyer, they should obtain clarification of paragraphs which are unclear and hear which points the lawyer is unhappy about.

It must be realised that indemnities concerning taxation matters are commonplace, and offer relatively little room for negotiation. In essence, the purchaser will require full recompense if unexpected tax liabilities arise for up to six years after legal completion.

Important issues to be negotiated are the maximum extent of the value of indemnity to be given and the *de minimis* limit, below which no claim can be pursued. Given the costs of litigation, it is in the interest of both parties to have a reasonably high *de minimis* limit.

Purchasers will not withdraw warranties or indemnities from the contract because the vendors say that everything is in order and therefore it would be superfluous to include them in the contract. Equally unacceptable will be the suggestion that a warranty or indemnity should be omitted because the purchasers are aware that it cannot be given because of known circumstances. They will require the vendors to reveal the matter in the disclosure statement.

After the initial meeting between the vendors and their lawyers to discuss the draft contract, it is desirable that the two sets of lawyers amend and agree as much of the contract as possible between themselves.

Supplementary agreements

Service contracts for the continued employment of certain directors will be written in the standard format used by the purchasing company. Negotiation is likely to be restricted mainly to the amount of salary, length of contract, and period of notice. When an earn-out deal is involved, the vendors should have a fixed term service contract up to three months after the end of the earn-out so that they can supervise the preparation of the final accounts.

Lease agreements should be relatively uncontentious in wording, compared with the importance of the purchase contract.

Due diligence process

It is recommended that the accountancy investigation is not scheduled, or allowed, to commence until there has been two or three days to consider the draft contract. It is unlikely, but does happen occasionally, that the contract contains items which had not been discussed and are completely unacceptable. One such example was a retention of 20 per cent of the purchase consideration for two years.

The accountancy investigation requires considerable time spent on company premises. The minimum is likely to be two people on site for a week, and could be much larger and longer for a sizeable and complex sale.

The investigating accountants will require answers to searching questions about the audited accounts, current year forecasts and future projections. The auditors should be able to handle issues arising from the statutory accounts, but not necessarily to explain the commercial realities behind the figures. So, detailed information will need to be provided internally. In some cases, it may be necessary and better to take the financial director into your confidence in order to deal directly with the investigating accountants. Otherwise, he or she is likely to conclude that the business is being sold by the flurry of questions being asked.

To minimise the time spent on site by investigating accountants, the vendors need to be well prepared. Even before Heads of Agreement are signed, you should obtain an information checklist from your own lawyers in order to commence compiling and collating the information required. As soon as Heads of Agreement are signed, you should ask the purchaser for their information checklist, but by then much of your preparatory work should be well under way.

The aim should be to deliver as much as possible of the information required to the investigating accountants so that it can be reviewed before they arrive, and so minimise the time spent on site. For a straightforward transaction, the information should be delivered in indexed, lever arch files. At least four copies will be required to give to the:

- investigating accountants;
- the acquirers lawyers;

- the vendors lawyers;

- and one must be retained by the vendors.

Any additional information or updated documents provided subsequently need to be dated and logged. This is not a counsel of perfection, it is vital good housekeeping for effective deal management.

Other due diligence experts may need to visit the premises, such as property surveyors or environmental consultants. Like the investigating accountants, they must be briefed how to announce themselves on arrival. Rumour and speculation by your staff are likely. A property surveyor who says on arrival *"I'm here to value the property"* would destroy confidentiality.

Accountants' report

Even though it is highly unusual for the vendors to be allowed to see the investigating accountants' report, it is worth knowing when it is expected. This should help to eliminate a possible excuse for delaying legal completion. Also, it enables contact to be made to check that the accountants' report is satisfactory, as was to be expected.

The purchasers may respond differently. In an extreme case, they may withdraw from the deal and only give a broad outline of their reasons. More often, the purchaser may seek to negotiate a lower price or to switch to an earn-out deal as a result of the investigation. This is the time for the vendors to demonstrate resolve.

If the vendors were honest and open when discussing the business with the purchasers prior to negotiation, then it should be possible to state that the items were known about previously. If important features were not outlined accurately or omitted, the vendors should expect re-negotiation, and if sufficiently serious, then the withdrawal of the purchaser.

A point worth making to purchasers is that accountants' reports tend to be critical by the nature of the exercise. Also, some accountancy firms have faced expensive litigation as a result of shortcomings not uncovered during their investigation, which makes them cautious when writing their report on the business.

Contract agreement

It is unlikely that the two sets of lawyers will be able to reach a final agreement of the whole draft contract without the intervention of the principals. There are likely to be at least a few material points to be resolved.

It is for this reason that it is advisable to reserve a date for a meeting to resolve any outstanding contractual matters. If this is not included as part of the timetable, the problem of people not being available for a meeting could delay legal completion.

Before the meeting takes place, it is important that the vendors have been briefed on the outstanding points and the differences of opinion which exist on each one. The principals and their advisers should be at the meeting, and it is important that sufficient time is available to negotiate an agreement on all outstanding points. Then, after the meeting, the lawyers can be left to amend and agree the wording of the contract.

Disclosure statement

The onus is on the vendors to disclose circumstances which breach the warranties given in the contract. This is done in the form of a disclosure statement, prepared by the vendors' lawyers based on information provided by them. Care must be taken to ensure that all relevant disclosures are made.

Some vendors regard the disclosure statement as unimportant and are tempted not to disclose things which could adversely affect the agreed deal. This is totally wrong. Information which is disclosed limits the effect of the warranties and prevents the acquirer litigating against the vendors because the information disclosed has become part of the contract. So vendors should make comprehensive disclosures, including copies of relevant correspondence and documents, which could amount to several lever arch files. Not to disclose any breach of a warranty is unthinkable, it is an invitation for the acquirer to litigate if it has material consequences.

Sometimes the lawyers do not present the disclosure statement until the day of legal completion. This can cause unwanted problems and delay on what should be an enjoyable day. The purchasers may find some parts of the disclosure statement too broad to be acceptable. This could lead to substantial rewriting of the disclosure statement, not to mention some harsh words being spoken, before legal completion takes place.

On the other hand, there is a case for presenting the disclosure statement at the final meeting to resolve any outstanding points when the principals are present. Knowledge of exactly what is to be disclosed, and the wording to be used, can make agreement of the outstanding points more easily reached. It has to be said, however, that opinions differ amongst experienced professionals on how best to handle disclosure statements.

Legal completion

Legal completion should be an enjoyable day for both sides. When a private company is sold, it marks the end of an era for the vendors. They are parting with an important slice of their lives.

Too often the day of legal completion is boring and tense. Boring because the lawyers may arrive at the same time as the principals, and then spend two or three hours sorting out the documentation and clearing up technical details. All of which should have been done before. It is worth asking the lawyers to arrive two or three hours earlier, if they feel it is necessary, in order to have everything ready before the vendors arrive.

Worse still, the disclosure statement may need some rewriting and there may be one or two contentious legal points still outstanding. This really does detract from the occasion of legal completion. At the final meeting to agree the outstanding points of difference remaining in the contract, both sets of lawyers should be asked to ensure a speedy and smooth legal completion meeting.

Lastly, a subjective comment. Midday is an excellent time to sign the documents for legal completion. Why? Because there is time for a celebratory glass of champagne or two before an enjoyable lunch with the purchasers – at their expense!

Executive summary

- A timetable to legal completion should be agreed at the end of the detailed negotiation meeting.

- Heads of Agreement are normally subject to contract, which means they are non-binding in most respects. While they are not essential, they are commonplace.

- Indemnities concerning all taxation matters are included in purchase contracts.

- The accountancy investigation should not be allowed to commence until the draft contract has been received.

- A meeting may be required, with the principals present, to resolve outstanding differences in the contract which the lawyers cannot agree upon.

- Care must be taken to give comprehensive and accurate information in the disclosure statement.

- Last-minute preparation needs to be done by the lawyers to ensure an acceptably short and enjoyable legal completion meeting.

TEN
How to eliminate losses before selling

It is surprising how often both listed groups and private companies choose to sell when the subsidiary or business is making a loss.

This is probably the worst possible time to sell. The best possible course of action is to turn the business back into profit and then to consider a sale. Not only may the business have proved unsaleable before, but a substantially higher price should be obtained. To convince prospective purchasers, however, is likely to require a profitable financial year, following a loss, and another year underway showing a robust forecast increase in profits. So it probably needs about two years to demonstrate effectively that a sustained turn-around has been achieved.

It is particularly difficult for the owner directors of a private company to achieve a turn-around because some painful decisions may have to be made. According to the scale of losses, a turn-around may demand one or more of the following:

- Some staff redundancies.

- Closure of an unprofitable branch office.

- Terminating unprofitable products or services.

- Recognising that an experienced chief executive must be recruited externally and given enough freedom to restore profitability.

- Worst of all, realising that at least one owner director may have to leave or retire for the business to survive.

In many ways it is easier for a group to turn-around a subsidiary because it should be able to transfer a proven executive to carry out the turn-around.

There is no time to lose. What is needed, however, is a proven framework for turning around a loss maker. Urgent and decisive action is essential. In a loss-making business, as with a road-accident victim, the first step is to stop the bleeding.

This is obvious and common sense. Unfortunately, too often the response is indecision and procrastination. In one group with a turnover of over £3 billion, analysis showed that the worst performing subsidiaries had produced a sizeable aggregate loss in each of the previous two years. These subsidiaries accounted for over a third of total group turnover, and the current year forecast showed little improvement for them; yet the group board displayed no sense of urgency to tackle the problem. Good results in the remainder of the group meant that overall performance was satisfactory, but it could have been much better.

Unless the chief executive of a loss-making subsidiary has a convincing plan to restore success as quickly as is possible in the particular circumstances which exist, he or she should be removed promptly. The problem is that people with a record of managing successful companies to achieve greater success often have no experience of turning round loss-making companies. The management style required is very different. In a successful company a newly appointed chief executive will take time before making significant changes, but in a turn-around situation the new person must make their impact felt from the first day.

The new chief executive needs to be full-time, and a substantial amount of overtime will be required initially. He or she will need the support of an experienced financial manager. If one does not exist within the business, then someone should be provided immediately, on a temporary secondment from elsewhere within the group if necessary.

A programme is necessary to ensure that progress is achieved quickly. An outline programme could be:

Day 1   Take financial control and make an impact.

Week 1   Deal urgently with any cash flow crisis which threatens survival.

Assess the financial performance in broad terms.

Initiate financial analysis as a basis for making short-term decisions.

Start to decide the level of initial cost reduction necessary.

Month 1   Investigate each area of the business.

Decide the level of cost reduction required in each function.

Ask departmental managers to make specific recommendations to achieve the cost reduction required.

Make preparations to announce the headcount reductions needed.

Carry out the headcount reduction needed and reassure the remaining staff.

Month 2   Initiate short-term profit improvement projects.

Set a budget for the remainder of the financial year.

Months 3 to 6 Begin to create the vision for future success.

Define major business development projects to create an adequate return on funds invested.

The first day

Urgency must be displayed at the outset. Financial control must be secured immediately. Initially, strict scrutiny will apply to:

- placing purchase orders;

- signing cheques;

- recruitment, including replacing people who leave; and

- foreign travel.

An impact needs to be made. Some items of avoidable and non-essential expense should be terminated immediately. If it is damaging the business, someone will complain. Examples where immediate cost reduction should be made include:

- Personal expenses – lavish meals, expensive hotels and first class travel should be replaced by a more modest approach. There should be no exceptions allowed. The chief executive must set a personal example.

- Temporary staff – all temporary staff should be terminated immediately unless they are revenue-earning or essential to serve the customer.

- Company cars – cars should be replaced only when the cost of repair becomes unacceptable.

- Discretionary expenses – plans for items such as re-equipping staff canteens, painting offices and other non-essential expenditure should be delayed until profitability has been restored.

The first week

If there is a cash flow crisis threatening the survival of the business immediate action must be taken. This may include:

- Using senior managers and partners to collect overdue debts by telephone call or personal visit wherever appropriate, concentrating on large amounts which can be received quickly.

- Negotiations with bankers and others to secure additional finance or an increased overdraft facility.

- Negotiations with tax authorities to avoid legal action for overdue payments and to agree a phased payment schedule, even though penal interest rates will be charged.

- Paying only those invoices necessary to avoid legal action and to ensure continuity of essential supplies and services.

- Seeking extended credit terms from major suppliers wherever appropriate.

Much of this action may only be needed temporarily.

The rest of the first week should be spent searching out the reasons for making a loss.

Sometimes the required financial analysis is not available to highlight the extent of the problem. In one turn-around situation, in the silicon chip industry, only out-of-date standard costs were available, the current actual product costs were not known. Falling prices caused by rapid technological change and surplus capacity elsewhere in the industry meant that some products were being sold for less than the standard product cost, on the assumption that at least a reasonable marginal profit was being made. An urgent and necessarily approximate marginal cost analysis showed that the market price for the best selling product had fallen below marginal cost. Every unit of this product which was sold increased the loss, so the more that were sold the bigger became the loss. Drastic and urgent action had to be taken.

Other problems may include a shortage of orders, inaccurate contract cost estimating, inefficient production, costly subcontract work and excessive overhead levels. A swift decision on the immediate level of cost reduction needs to be made.

The first month

The remainder of the first month should be spent assessing each aspect of the business at first hand. By the end of the month, preparation for any headcount reduction required should have been made. If the law requires a minimum period of notice to be given before redundancies can be made, the need for urgency is even greater.

Sales

The sales department, rather than marketing, is the recommended starting point for examining the business, as it is closest to the customer. To find out the true sales situation, there is no substitute for accompanying sales staff on customer visits. One can quickly find out both customer reaction and sales effectiveness.

The next area to examine should be the sale-support functions, such as the sales office, estimating department and after-sales service. Aspects to be examined should include:

- What credit status checks are made on prospective customers and what is the level of bad debts?

- How accurate are product, service and contract cost estimates?

- How competitive are prices, quantity discounts and payment terms?

- What are the authority and basis for quoting non-standard prices?

- How quickly and professionally are quotations submitted?

- How quick is delivery? Are sales being lost because of long delivery periods?

- What is the level of out-of-stock situations?

- What is the level of complaints and warranty claims, and how well are they handled?

- How quickly and effectively are telephone calls, emails and correspondence acted upon?

Marketing

Marketing should be examined next. The knowledge gained from the sales operations should be of valuable help in assessing marketing effectiveness.

It is particularly easy for people to confuse work and results in marketing. Factual answers should be obtained to searching questions such as:

- How does the department measure its own effectiveness?

- What tangible results and contributions have been achieved?

- How is the effectiveness of advertising, exhibitions and other promotional activities measured?

- What is known in detail about the market and competition

Manufacturing, delivery of services, distribution and administration should be examined next. Questions to be asked include the following:

Manufacturing or service delivery

- How can we reduce product or service delivery costs without additional capital expenditure?

- What is needed to reduce product or service costs significantly?

- How can reject and wastage levels be reduced?

- How can product or service quality and reliability be increased without additional cost?

- Which production bottlenecks needs to be overcome?

- How can delivery times be shortened with additional facilities?

- What small outlays of expenditure would produce substantial profit improvement speedily?

- How can raw-material, work-in-progress and finished-goods stocks be reduced without losing profitable sales opportunities?

- What surplus equipment and redundant stocks should be sold off?

Distribution

- How can distribution costs be reduced internally or outsourced?

- How can deliveries be speeded up?

- What are the levels of damaged goods and items returned?

- How else can customer service be improved?

- How are peak-period requirements dealt with?

Administration

- What would happen if we stopped doing this task, or scrapped the whole department?

- Why is it done daily and not weekly, or weekly instead of monthly, etc?

- Could it be done less expensively in another department or location or outsourced at lower cost?

- What jobs are being left undone, to the detriment of the business?

Research and development

Research and development is probably, but not necessarily, the last department to be examined. Questions to be asked include:

- What proportion of the total budget is spent on:
  - fundamental research?
  - new product development?
  - improvements to existing products?

- What is the status of each current project?

- What are the market, commercial and financial arguments for continuing each project?

- What projects are planned to start in the foreseeable future?

- What tangible results have come from the department in recent years, and what failures?

At the end of this review of the company, the chief executive should decide upon the level of cost reduction to be achieved in each department. A common percentage cost reduction in each department may appear to be equitable, but it is almost certainly inappropriate.

The head of each function should be asked to make specific proposals for the people to be dismissed and other cost reductions to be made, for approval by the chief executive. Speed and confidentiality are important, as rumours and anxiety are inevitable.

The second month

Redundancies should be announced simultaneously across the whole company, for people need to be assured and to believe that further redundancies will be unnecessary. A second round of redundancies is likely to cause lasting damage to morale.

Departmental managers should submit concise written profit improvement plans for immediate implementation, and give an estimate of the effect on current-year profits.

Revised budgets should be prepared quickly for the remainder of the current year. The chief executive will need to review and approve each department budget to ensure that the level of achievement proposed is sufficiently demanding.

The financial analysis which has been done will enable the monthly sales figures required to achieve a break-even position to be calculated. Every manager must be aware of the figure and a target month agreed upon as the deadline for exceeding the sales figure required to break even.

It must be realised, however, that eliminating losses is only the first stage of a successful turn-around. The goal must be to achieve an adequate return on the total funds invested in the business. Eliminating losses is usually the easier and quicker task. Selecting a few key tasks to be done urgently, simply and outstandingly well is often sufficient to eliminate losses. To achieve a satisfactory return on investment in a turn-around situation may require major new initiatives to be taken, particularly if there is surplus capacity in the market sector.

Months three to six

By now the worst of the upheaval and disruption should be out of the way. No time must be lost in building future success. A vision statement should be written with the total commitment of the management team. Their major business development projects should be identified, and personal account-abilities assigned, as the means of translating the vision into tangible achievement.

The vision statement and business development projects need to be addressed before budget preparation for the next financial year begins. The budget process should be particularly rigorous in order to provide a clearly thought-out operating plan for the coming financial year. The management team must realise that the agreed budget represents a collective cabinet commitment to achieve the profit and cash flow budgets.

Two of the most valuable assets for the chief executive are enthusiasm and belief. He must exude them every day, however tough the going becomes. Gradually his belief and enthusiasm will be shared by the rest of the management team.

Owner directors of private companies may find the systematic approach to business turn-around set out above, to be draconian and brutal; so be it. The fact remains, however, that some decisive action is needed quickly to avoid further erosion of shareholder value and to ensure business survival. At the very least, owner directors should work through the systematic approach outlined and implement those actions which they find palatable.

Executive summary

- Take control and make an impact on the first day.

- Attack a cash flow crisis during the first week.

- Assess each department and decide the initial cost reduction required during the first month.

- Carry out any headcount reduction needed during the second month.

- Develop a vision for future success and define major business development projects during the second quarter.

- Recognise that approximate financial analysis done quickly is much more valuable than waiting for accurate figures to be produced.

Thorogood publishing

Thorogood publishes a wide range of books, reports, special briefings, psychometric tests and videos. Listed below is a selection of key titles.

Desktop Guides

The marketing strategy desktop guide	*Norton Paley* • £16.99
The sales manager's desktop guide	*Mike Gale and Julian Clay* • £16.99
The company director's desktop guide	*David Martin* • £16.99
The credit controller's desktop guide	*Roger Mason* • £16.99
The company secretary's desktop guide	*Roger Mason* • £16.99
The finance and accountancy desktop guide	*Ralph Tiffin* • £16.99
The commercial engineer's desktop guide	*Tim Boyce* • £16.99
The training manager's desktop guide	*Eddie Davies* • £16.99
The PR practitioner's desktop guide	*Caroline Black* • £16.99
Win new business - the desktop guide	*Susan Croft* • £16.99

Masters in Management

Mastering business planning and strategy	*Paul Elkin* • £14.99
Mastering financial management	*Stephen Brookson* • £14.99
Mastering leadership	*Michael Williams* • £14.99
Mastering marketing	*Ian Ruskin-Brown* • £16.99
Mastering negotiations	*Eric Evans* • £14.99
Mastering people management	*Mark Thomas* • £14.99
Mastering personal and interpersonal skills	*Peter Haddon* • £14.99
Mastering project management	*Cathy Lake* • £14.99

Business Action Pocketbooks

Edited by David Irwin

Building your business pocketbook	£6.99
Developing yourself and your staff pocketbook	£6.99
Finance and profitability pocketbook	£6.99
Managing and employing people pocketbook	£6.99
Sales and marketing pocketbook	£6.99

Managing projects and operations pocketbook	£6.99
Effective business communications pocketbook	£6.99
PR techniques that work	*Edited by Jim Dunn* • £6.99
Adair on leadership	*Edited by Neil Thomas* • £6.99

Other titles

The complete guide to debt recovery	*Roger Mason* • £12.99
The John Adair handbook of management and leadership	*Edited by Neil Thomas* • £12.99
The inside track to successful management	*Dr Gerald Kushel* • £12.99
The pension trustee's handbook (3rd edition)	*Robin Ellison* • £25
Boost your company's profits	*Barrie Pearson* • £12.99
Negotiate to succeed	*Julie Lewthwaite* • £12.99
The management tool kit	*Sultan Kermally* • £10.99
Working smarter	*Graham Roberts-Phelps* • £14.99
Test your management skills	*Michael Williams* • £15.99
The art of headless chicken management	*Elly Brewer and Mark Edwards* • £6.99
Everything you need for an NVQ in management	*Julie Lewthwaite* • £22.99
Customer relationship management	*Graham Roberts-Phelps* • £14.99
Sales management and organisation	*Peter Green* • £10.99
Telephone tactics	*Graham Roberts-Phelps* • £10.99
Companies don't succeed people do!	*Graham Roberts-Phelps* • £12.99
Inspiring leadership	*John Adair* • £15.99
The book of Me	*Barrie Pearson and Neil Thomas* • £14.99
The complete guide to debt recovery	*Roger Mason* • £12.99
Dynamic practice development	*Kim Tasso* • £19.99
Gurus on business strategy	*Tony Grundy* • £14.99
The concise Adair on leadership	*Edited by Neil Thomas* • £9.99
The concise time management and personal development	*Adair and Melanie Allen* • £9.99
Successful selling solutions	*Julian Clay* • £12.99
Gurus on marketing	*Sultan Kermally* • £14.99

The concise Adair on communication and presentation skills

Edited by Neil Thomas • £9.99

High performance consulting skills   *Mark Thomas* • £15.99

Developing and managing talent   *Sultan Kermally* • £14.99

Thorogood also has an extensive range of reports and special briefings which are written specifically for professionals wanting expert information.

For a full listing of all Thorogood publications, or to order any title, please call Thorogood Customer Services on 020 7749 4748 or fax on 020 7729 6110. Alternatively view our website at **www.thorogood.ws**.

Focused on developing your potential

Falconbury, the sister company to Thorogood publishing, brings together the leading experts from all areas of management and strategic development to provide you with a comprehensive portfolio of action-centred training and learning.

We understand everything managers and leaders need to be, know and do to succeed in today's commercial environment. Each product addresses a different technical or personal development need that will encourage growth and increase your potential for success.

- Practical public training programmes
- Tailored in-company training
- Coaching
- Mentoring
- Topical business seminars
- Trainer bureau/bank
- Adair Leadership Foundation

The most valuable resource in any organisation is its people; it is essential that you invest in the development of your management and leadership skills to ensure your team fulfil their potential. Investment into both personal and professional development has been proven to provide an outstanding ROI through increased productivity in both you and your team. Ultimately leading to a dramatic impact on the bottom line.

With this in mind Falconbury have developed a comprehensive portfolio of training programmes to enable managers of all levels to develop their skills in leadership, communications, finance, people management, change management and all areas vital to achieving success in today's commercial environment.

What Falconbury can offer you?

- Practical applied methodology with a proven results
- Extensive bank of experienced trainers
- Limited attendees to ensure one-to-one guidance
- Up to the minute thinking on management and leadership techniques
- Interactive training
- Balanced mix of theoretical and practical learning
- Learner-centred training
- Excellent cost/quality ratio

Falconbury In-Company Training

Falconbury are aware that a public programme may not be the solution to leadership and management issues arising in your firm. Involving only attendees from your organisation and tailoring the programme to focus on the current challenges you face individually and as a business may be more appropriate. With this in mind we have brought together our most motivated and forward thinking trainers to deliver tailored in-company programmes developed specifically around the needs within your organisation.

All our trainers have a practical commercial background and highly refined people skills. During the course of the programme they act as facilitator, trainer and mentor, adapting their style to ensure that each individual benefits equally from their knowledge to develop new skills.

Falconbury works with each organisation to develop a programme of training that fits your needs.

Mentoring and coaching

Developing and achieving your personal objectives in the workplace is becoming increasingly difficult in today's constantly changing environment. Additionally, as a manager or leader, you are responsible for guiding colleagues towards the realisation of their goals. Sometimes it is easy to lose focus on your short and long-term aims.

Falconbury's one-to-one coaching draws out individual potential by raising self-awareness and understanding, facilitating the learning and perform-ance development that creates excellent managers and leaders. It builds renewed self-confidence and a strong sense of 'can-do' competence, contributing significant benefit to the organisation. Enabling you to focus your energy on developing your potential and that of your colleagues.

Mentoring involves formulating winning strategies, setting goals, monitoring achievements and motivating the whole team whilst achieving a much improved work life balance.

Falconbury – Business Legal Seminars

Falconbury Business Legal Seminars specialises in the provision of high quality training for legal professionals from both in-house and private practice internationally.

The focus of these events is to provide comprehensive and practical training on current international legal thinking and practice in a clear and informative format.

Event subjects include, drafting commercial agreements, employment law, competition law, intellectual property, managing an in-house legal department and international acquisitions.

For more information on all our services please contact Falconbury on +44 (0) 20 7729 6677 or visit the website at: www.falconbury.co.uk.